The Seven Deadly Virtues

Father & Son: A Personal Biography of
Senator Frank Church of Idaho by His Son

The Devil & Dr. Church: A Guide to Hell
for Atheists and True Believers

Entertaining Angels: A Guide to Heaven
for Atheists and True Believers

The Essential Tillich: An Anthology of the Writings
of Paul Tillich

The Macmillan Book of Earliest Christian Prayers
(*with Terrence Mulry*)

The Seven Deadly Virtues

A Guide to Purgatory for Atheists and True Believers

F. Forrester Church

1817

Harper & Row, Publishers, San Francisco

Cambridge, Hagerstown, New York, Philadelphia, Washington
London, Mexico City, São Paulo, Singapore, Sydney

Parts of this book have been adapted from articles published originally by the author in *The Chicago Tribune, The Boston Globe, The Church and State Quarterly,* and *Religious Humanism.*

FIRST EDITION

Library of Congress Cataloging-in-Publication Data

Church, F. Forrester.
  The seven deadly virtues.

  Bibliography: p.
  1. Purgatory—Anecdotes, facetiae, satire, etc. 2. Virtues—Anecdotes, facetiae, satire, etc. I. Title.
BT842.C48   1988   236'.5   87-45729
ISBN 0-06-061373-4

88 89 90 91 92 HC 10 9 8 7 6 5 4 3 2 1

To John Buehrens

Contents

Preface

Two years ago, my wife took our daughter on a week-long junket to California, leaving the men in the family to their own devices. When she returned, Amy was surprised to find the refrigerator so full. That was because my son and I lived it up. Nightly we dined at the restaurant across the street, a dive specializing in grilled-cheese sandwiches and raisin bran for dinner.

One evening, while supping together in this splendid establishment, Twig said to me, "You know, Daddy, I believe in God, but I don't believe in dinosaurs."

Here I made a theological mistake. I plunged into bones. For a minute or two he listened distractedly, then dismissed my argument with a toss of his head. "I believe in God," Twig said, "because God is everywhere. Dinosaurs are extinct."

For dinosaurs, substitute "the seven (deadly) virtues," and that, in a nutshell, is the thesis of this book.

With it I complete *A Humane Comedy,* my trilogy on heaven, hell, and purgatory. In *The Devil & Dr. Church,* I defined the devil as "evil disguised as good."* In *Entertaining Angels,* I described angels as "goodness disguised." If they came wrapped in packages, we would almost always choose the wrong one.

Here both definitions continue to pertain, for purgatory

---

*Sources for quoted material begin on page 105.

is heaven and hell at once. One eminent divine wrote that, "If purgatory is a species of hell as regards suffering, it is even more a species of paradise as regards heavenly love and sweetness." But that's not always the case. Much "suffering" is heaven-sent, casting shadows of happiness, whereas "love" (when destructive of its object) and "sweetness" (which may rot the tooth that savors it) are often numbered in the devil's arsenal.

In my tour of purgatory, despite my penchant for excursion, I bow to a previous guide, one who has done more than any other to make purgatory a respectable topic of theological and literary reflection. In Dante's *Purgatorio,* the seven cornices leading from lower to upper purgatory are each classified according to one of the seven deadly sins. Himself guided by Virgil, Dante first visits the proud, envious, and wrathful in lower purgatory; then the slothful in middle purgatory; and finally the covetous, gluttonous, and lustful at the top of the mountain in upper purgatory. In each case the punishment reflects those that torment the lost souls in Dante's *Inferno.* As Dorothy Sayers points out, "The pains of Purgatory are in themselves very like those of Hell, and some of them are but little lighter. The penitent Proud, like the impenitent Hypocrites, ceaseless walk their appointed round bowed down by heavy weights. . . . The sole transforming difference is in the mental attitude of the sufferers."

As you take my guided tour of purgatory, you will discover that in some respects things haven't changed all that much over the past five centuries. Purgatory is still that place of purification where those being saved do not begrudge but rather welcome their pains as emblems of their reunion with God. But there is one important difference. It lies in the nature of the crimes for which we must do penance. If Dante's seven gates brandish the seven deadly sins, mine replace them with the seven deadly virtues. I deeply believe that today we are far more likely to be unwitting victims of our virtues than our sins.

I am speaking here of crimes committed under the banners of prudence and justice, temperance and fortitude, even faith, hope, and love. The seven deadly virtues are not deadly according to nature. By definition, virtue is good. The four philosophical and three theological virtues are only deadly when malpracticed, but then devastatingly so, for they lend the appearance of nobility to evil. As one great theologian, John Scotus Erigena, wrote in the ninth century, "No vice is found but in the shadow of some virtue." Those of us who face some chosen light (justice, faith, or whatever) may be blinded by it. Basking in its reflected glow—"we are just, we are faithful"—we may fail to notice that as long as we face the light, we cannot see our shadow. Blinded by our virtue, we forget that we *have* a shadow. And when we forget this, we become dangerous.

Shakespeare wrote that, "Our crimes would despair if they were not cherished by our virtues." As it is, our virtues not only cherish, but also camouflage our crimes. In this age of interdependence, the salvation (health or wholeness) of anyone on this planet is in growing measure dependent upon the salvation of his or her neighbors. Yet, the most punishable of crimes, sins against the earth and against humankind, are among those for which we are as likely to be unwittingly proud as justifiably punished.

If all this strikes you as a bit overripe in paradox, I can only reply that almost everything these days has to be turned upside down before we can begin to understand it.

We are a little like the early immigrants to Australia. As one witness reported concerning the inversion of language there, "*Evil* was literally called *good,* and good, *evil*—the well-disposed man was branded *wicked,* whilst the leader in monstrous vice was styled *virtuous.*" In America today, "wicked" and "bad" are positive adjectives in adolescent lingo, but "good" and "virtue" still retain their old cachet.

All the more reason to beware.

I begin my exploration of the seven deadly virtues by investigating purgatory itself, starting with definitions, and then testing the power of its purifying fires to burn away our self-deceit. Then I leave purgatory for a time, turning to the virtues themselves. Upon attending to the perils they present in their modern attenuated, privatistic form, I shall test the possibilities of a postindividualistic ethic, one grounded in principles of interdependency as reflected by new metaphors for the nature of God. Finally, I offer a vision of pentecost in purgatory, when the tongues of fire descend upon our heads, and each of us can understand what the other is saying, though we speak in different languages and even of different truths.

My subject is not purgatory after life, but purgatory before death. In this I follow St. Catherine of Genoa. To paraphrase her *Treatise on Purgatory,* she presents purgatory as "the projection beyond of that mystical purgation which also takes place in this world in souls open to God's action." She speaks of "the holy soul, still in the flesh, placed in the purgatory of God's burning love so that it might, at the time of death, go straight to God. In this way one is to understand how it is with the souls in purgatory, abiding content in the fire of divine love."

As with my last two books, this essay on purgatory is

part of a continuing effort to remythologize humanism. For too long, those of us with skeptical temperaments have contented ourselves with a false distinction, namely that anything not susceptible to investigation according to the canons of rationality is by definition irrational. We entertain as verifiable and therefore worthy of our attention only those things we can subject to recognized proofs of evidence. Everything else, including the devil and angels, heaven, hell, purgatory, and even God, we relegate as figments to the irrational realm.

Together with our children, many leading scientists are far ahead of us in this regard. Some of the most recent discoveries in mathematics and particle physics make no apparent sense, at least not according to known canons of rationality. In probing the mysteries of the universe and the mind, researchers on the cutting edge of knowledge find themselves moving freely between the rational and trans-rational realms. As physicist Alan Lightman writes, "Of all people today, I think scientists have the deepest faith in the unseen world. The greater the scientist, the deeper his faith." Even allowing for hyperbole, where does that leave the poor camp-followers who believe in science but don't know anything about it? Sadly, having traded in God for truth, they are left with neither.

Much religion today continues to be irrational, of course. Claims of scriptural inerrancy, virgin birth, and creation science with the scriptures and not the cosmos as primary evidence, are indeed irrational. But an equally serious charge may be leveled at liberal religion, especially in its most radical (which is to say reactionary) form. In our principled flight from irrationality, we have almost wholly lost sight of the transrational realm, where reason is not rejected but rather transcended. This is the realm of myth and parable, poetry and paradox, symbol and salvation. Wholeness cannot be achieved until the two realms—the realms of sign and symbol, of fact and fancy—are explored as one.

So when the irrationalist says that there are miracles because the Bible tells me so, and the rationalist replies there are no such thing as miracles, both are wrong. All life is a miracle. And when they cite conflicting authorities to prove the existence or nonexistence of God, their exercises are in vain. God is not God's name. God is our name for that which is greater than all and yet present in each— the life force, the ground of being, being itself. So defined, God is beyond knowing or naming; in our accustomed ways of seeing, both too close and too far away for us to see.

Yet, if explorations of the transrational realm do not yield trophies we can bring home and tack on our walls, we do return from such journeys blessed with new eyes to glimpse the divine amidst the ordinary, and new ears to hear the still, small voice. Then sight becomes miracle and hearing too. No further proofs are necessary, save one, when having heard and having seen, we translate our very lives into evidences of God.

My own definition of religion is a simple one. Religion is our human response to the dual reality of being alive and having to die. We are all religious creatures. As with those responding to Barnum's barkers, the box we put our coin in will always contain a prize. Some may not be instant winners. If one brands our life with purpose, another burns a hole in our hand. No matter. We can't avoid taking chances on life's meaning, and meaning comes from the chances that we take. Regardless of our luck, the promise of purgatory is still ours.

Just as in poker. If played right, any card holds at least some promise; and even the best hand, if everyone else folds, is good for nothing.

One final word. Though respectful of special interest theology, I am a universalist. With Origen, the first great student of purgatory, I prefer to imagine that all of us have the prospect of being purified in an ongoing process of baptism by fire, rather than selectively redeemed according to our virtues, or condemned to an eternity of anything by virtue of our sins.

I thank Clayton Carlson, vice president and publisher of Harper & Row, for his continuing (if often bemused) encouragement; my gracious editor, Roy M. Carlisle; my friends Deborah Berger and James Jarnagin; and Terry Mulry of Harvard Divinity School, who helped me with the research for this book. I wrote it on a visit to one of the more pleasant precincts of this earthly purgatory, Laguna Niguel, California, hosted by the generosity of my parents-in-law, Gordon and Nina Furth, and was able to complete it due to the patience of my family, Amy, Twig, and Nina, who by now are well practiced in putting up with my "virtuous" eccentricity of writing while on vacation.

I dedicate this book to my colleague in purgatory, John Buehrens, who suggested, among other things, its title. After a tremendously successful tenure as senior minister, last year John left one of the largest churches in our denomination to join his ministry to mine at the Unitarian Church of All Souls in New York City. For this I am immensely grateful. Though pronounced by all our colleagues as at best a risky venture, we tend to be amused rather than irritated by one another's idiosyncrasies, which is my definition of a good, working marriage.

1. The Promise of Purgatory

Of that second realm, which purifies
Man's spirit of its soilure, will I sing.

DANTE

And so, Mr. M'Rory, you are really such a superstitious blockhead as to believe in purgatory, are you?

SYDNEY OWENSON MORGAN

Legend has it that when St. Patrick visited County Donegal, Ireland, brandishing a muscular gospel well suited to vanquish the tired remnants of a once thriving Druidical cultus, Christ appeared to him in a vision. Among those places holy to the Druids was a dark cave on the tiny island of Lough Derg. Rumored to be the mouth of hell, and altar-place for dark priestcraft worked by Druid elders in the ancient days, no one dared to approach this cave.

"Go there," Christ said to Patrick. "Enter the cave. Then return to the people with word of what you've seen. Great wonders will be revealed to you."

His followers valiantly tried to dissuade Patrick from accepting Christ's dare. Druidical lore had it that anyone who entered the mouth of hell would not return. Even newly baptized Christians, protected by the seal of Christ, lacked the temerity to test their faith against the spell of Druid magic. But Patrick would not be moved. He perceived correctly that this single act of valor, itself a reenactment of the victories of Yahweh over the priests of Baal, would do more to remove the veil of superstition than a thousand sermons.

He set sail at nightfall for Lough Derg to enter the mouth of hell.

All night long Patrick crouched in a damp, cold chamber deep within the cave. Just before daybreak his eyes opened upon a miraculous sight: the torments of hell and the ecstasy of heaven juxtaposed in a single image. *Loca purgatoria ostendit Deus*—"God showed him the places of Purgatory."

If, as scholars vow, Saint Patrick's Purgatory in Lough Derg, once the mouth of hell but henceforth a place of penitential pilgrimage for Christians, has no connection with the saint, it hardly matters. Legends need not be based on fact to be grounded in truth. The truth revealed in this legend is that purgatory isn't someplace halfway between hell and heaven. It is heaven and hell at once.

A later pilgrim, Sir Owen—who lived to tell, as some did not, of his own experience in St. Patrick's Purgatory— adds an important dimension to its lore. Upon returning from an extended period of fasting within the cave, he testified to the same bewildering admixture of heaven and hell. According to one report,

Light and darkness passed before Owen's eyes in strange comminglement. At last the movement was withheld, and he saw an endless throng of faithful souls kneeling in prayer and supplication. As far as his eyes could reach stretched the wonderful company. Their bodies seemed to tremble in an unseen flame like the fields that quiver in the heat of summer, and no wind blowing through them. At first they seemed to keep a fearful silence. Then there fell on Owen's ears a low and piteous cry, as if it were the sweet impatience of a child in pain. Over their yearning desolation brooded the shadow of an infinite happiness.

Here purgatory is riddled with paradox: light and darkness commingling strangely, with shadows of happiness playing upon a field bright with desolation, luminous with the fire of yearning, the very flames that incinerate simultaneously being flames that purify. This rich symbolism suggests something about the meaning of purgatory that has been all but lost. Purgatory is not so much a place of punishment, but rather a place of purification. It is a place where people suffer well in order to be saved.

Here, as in most renderings of purgatory, fire is the primary symbol. This image derives from the fire of judgment, which accompanies many of God's acts in the Jewish scriptures, and is promised in the New Testament as that which will separate human gold from dross in the final reckoning. Fire offers a panoply of symbolic nuance. It illumines, warms, incinerates, purifies. As a symbol of judgment, the latter two images are particularly apt. Fire discriminates between substances, turning some to ash, while tempering and perfecting others.

Origen, who believed in purgatory but not in hell, was graphic in his description of the fires of judgment burning in purgatory. "This fire consumes not the creature, but what the creature has himself built. . . . It is manifest that the fire destroys the wood of our transgressions, and then returns to us the reward of our good works."

The fire in purgatory is not the fire of hell; it is the fire of heaven. Our word "purify" (related to the word "pyre") stems from the Greek root for fire. It means literally "to manufacture by fire, to make more perfect by testing in flames." The fires of purgatory are not fires of punishment, but fires of purification.

The problem with purgatory as popularly understood is that heaven is missing. The fires of purification are perceived as fires of punishment. The blessing seems a curse.

This is especially true in common parlance. For instance, when Beaumont and Fletcher write, "There is no other purgatory but a woman," they are not bearing witness to women's power to cleanse men of their sins, any more than is the old adage, "Marriage with strife is this world's purgatory," intended to suggest that we perfect our marriages by adding a little strife to them.

Such popular misunderstandings color purgatory with a prejudicial pen. This is the first hurdle confronting one who aspires to reintroduce purgatory into the late-twentieth-century theological lexicon. But there is another, even more nettlesome obstacle: sectarian scruples, particularly among Protestants. After all, we Protestants are not supposed to believe in purgatory.

I must admit that the Catholic doctrine of purgatory has no scriptural basis, but surely this should not prove insurmountable. After all, the trinity has no scriptural basis either. Most Protestants haven't been daunted by that.

Remember, imagination is to theology as rain is to a garden. It lifts things into view that before were hidden, and keeps freshening them until they flourish. I speak as a Unitarian who finds the trinity a far more subtle and evocative metaphor for God than undifferentiated, nonmodal oneness. Being one who treasures such contradictions as signs that one's beliefs are unlikely to prove dangerous to others, I have no difficulty in suggesting to fellow Protestants that the time has arrived for us to overcome our scruples about purgatory, and plunge into its bright shadows in search of entry to the commonwealth of God.

Besides, the real reason purgatory was dropped by the reformers in the sixteenth century was not that purgatory had no scriptural basis. It had instead to do with corruptions of the indulgence system—itself a corruption of the original doctrine of purgatory—whereby people were enticed to give money to the church in order to purchase masses for the liberation of "poor" dead souls.

In fact, when in 1517 Archbishop Albert of Mainz appointed a Dominican monk, Johann Tetzel, to sell indulgences, it was the latter's unprecedented success in the soul-brokering business that prompted Martin Luther to nail his Ninety-five Theses to the church door at Wittenberg. Luther's passion may also have been fired by the perverse little rhyme that Hans Sachs ascribed to Tetzel: "When in the box the money rings, the soul from Purgatory springs."

Admittedly, there are pre-Christian precedents for this practice. In the second century B.C.E., after Judas Maccabeus scored his great victory on the field near Adullam, he discovered that his fallen soldiers had taken out a little bad insurance on their souls by wearing pagan amulets into battle. This, not surprisingly, constituted a breach of Mosaic law, and Judas, who was among the first to subscribe to the doctrine of resurrection, feared that his men would not receive their heavenly reward. So he raised a collection of twelve thousand drachmas, and sent it to Jerusalem as an expiatory sacrifice to atone for the fallen soldiers' sin. This is the first historical record of indulgences being secured. It is also the only citation for such a practice to be found, albeit apocryphally, in the Bible (2 Maccabees 12:39–46).

If common usage inverts the true meaning of purgatory (by replacing the connotation of purification with that of punishment), the indulgence system subverts it (by preempting the process by which a soul is cleansed). According to Dante, that moment comes when we feel ourselves to be purged and sound. It is a moment of recognition, not bestowed from without but confirmed from within.

A similar experience is recorded by Evelyn Underhill in her depiction of mystical union with God in this life, when a person reaches the point where "the new life has triumphed [and] mortification is at an end. The mystics always know when this moment comes. Often an inner voice then warns them to lay their active penances aside."

If we follow such clues as these, dismissing from mind the more negative and misleading connotations of purgatory, we shall perhaps begin to recover its redemptive promise as a metaphor for the cleansing of human souls along the road to God.

This road does not begin at death. Though we may spend a lifetime unaware that we are following it, it begins at birth. Whether purgatory continues after death remains a mystery. Taking the approach of the knight in Chaucer's *Canterbury Tales,*

> I have no doubt that it may well be so.
> I leave the answer for divines to tell,
> But that there's pain on earth I know too well.

Here I too shall stick with earthly pain—that which we know well—leaving the questions of pain after life to those who fashion themselves diviners of such things. Yet, regardless of venue, the nature of purgatory remains unchanged. Its promise is not to ease our pain, but to invest it with meaning. I think it was Archibald MacLeish who once said, "Our task, like Job's, is to learn through suffering how to love."

Not that any suffering will do. By itself to suffer is insufficient. Not only is much suffering self-inflicted and therefore unnecessary, but every unnecessary burden we bear burdens the world. We cannot carry anyone else on our shoulders when we are bent to the point of breaking under our own dead weight.

This reminds me of my student days, when I wore the furrowed brow of an angry existentialist. Back then I took myself very seriously indeed. I recall being particularly enamored of Albert Camus's statement that the only serious question is whether or not we should choose to continue to live.

Life is difficult. No one questions that. And the price we finally pay for life is death. But I have long since come to recognize that the ultimate question is not whether we should choose to continue living. In fact, the only question that really matters is this: Can we live in such a way that our lives will prove to be worth dying for?

When we accept the pledge of salvation by freely embracing the disciplines of purgatory, the first rite we are called upon to practice is the rite of purification. Initially this adds to our pain, but it lessens our burden by investing our pain with meaning. That which purifies also incinerates, but this too is good. If carried out in the holy precincts of purgatory, what the fires destroy in any such purge of ourselves are those things that separate us from our neighbors and God.

This is no simple matter. One doesn't just up and say with Shakespeare's Falstaff, "I'll purge, and leave sack, and live cleanly, as a nobleman should do." In fact, many a self-styled virtuous nobleman might better find his way to God by inverting these instructions until he discovers some measure of kinship between himself and other sinners. Until he manages this, he will remain aloof from the divine blandishments of purgatory.

In purgatory, spiritual discipline is spiritual refreshment, difficult but satisfying, like chipping off layers of paint to recover the natural wood. Outside purgatory, spiritual discipline is just another variety of punishment. It both strips us of our humanity and robs us from the world.

Here is where the doctrine of this-worldly purgatory is so telling. Purgatory is heaven and hell at once, here and now, shadows of happiness, bright fields of desolation, both of which remind us that, despite our pain—in fact, because of it—we're already saved and therefore have saving work to do before we die. Unlike tattered desert or garret creatures, pilgrims in purgatory are not expatriates from the world. They are patriots of the commonwealth of God.

This commonwealth is established first on earth, not in heaven. We earthlings are its stewards as well as its servants. All are partners here. Entry comes when we open ourselves to the promise of salvation, and accept the shared suffering that this promise entails.

I admit, it may be possible through a regimen of prayer, abstinence, and disengagement from worldly doings and striving, to attain to a kind of spiritual remove. One can always set up tent as a mystical cowboy, a lone gun, aloof, apart, abstracted from the world.

In fact, I know it's possible. I even tried it once.

Seventeen years ago, I was intern minister at Stanford University's Memorial Church. For six months I followed a strict ascetic regimen. I went to bed at one and awakened at five, spent each morning drinking Lapsang Soochong tea and reading Greek philosophy, and every afternoon serving as guru and guide to a few ragtail disciplines. Evenings I listened to Mahler and read Milton, the two primary sources for my budding eschatological vision.

I grew a long red beard, got a crew cut, lost thirty pounds, and collapsed. It was very dramatic. I was positive that I'd contracted consumption or some equally romantic nineteenth-century disease.

My wife was not impressed.

Neither was the doctor, a Stanford G.P. well practiced in the treatment of psychosomatic illness. I can still remember how scornful she was. She said that I had been behaving like an idiot. There was absolutely nothing wrong with me that a little more sleep and a little less tea would not instantly cure. She also told me that she never wanted to see me again. I never wanted to see her again either, so I cast myself from grace.

This was mock-purgatory, of course. Like anyone addicted by endorphins to running farther and farther every day, the high is real but its results are dysfunctional. One is left with splintered ankles, or a splintered soul.

This is true of all individualistic pyrotechnics, spiritual and otherwise. With rare exceptions, the fire devoted to perfecting technique ultimately incinerates that which we are trying to purify. It may be impressive, but such virtue is ultimately deadly. When we pursue perfection, either of body or soul, not only do we run out of time for our imperfect neighbors, but in a strange, sad way, we even run out of time for ourselves. As is the case on every field of individual combat, here the gates of purgatory are closed.

If we are looking for a bridge to take us there more directly, a far better model is motherhood: Heaven and hell at once, daily sacrifices made on behalf of children, each of whom holds the proxy of God.

I am a fool to bring this up. No unregenerate male should. Yet among my experiences in purgatory, my limited stint as a mother is among the most telling.

This is not a subject I preach on, by the way, though once I almost made that mistake. Having spent the better part of one day a week as primary care giver to my children, I thought I was acquainted with the basics.

I was wrong.

This was brought home to me with chastening effect when my wife, Amy, contracted pneumonia. She fell ill when we were on a family vacation. At first, my sacrifice was limited to playing with our children on the beach, a sandy job but someone had to do it. When we returned to New York and discovered the serious nature of her illness, things changed abruptly. I was humbled by reality.

Since our home was filled with dust due to recent construction, the doctor banished Amy to a luxurious convalescence with close friends. Let me tell you about my month with the children.

I did quite well, for about two days. By the middle of the first week, my then three-year-old daughter, Nina, and five-year-old son, Twig, had taken charge. From that point on, together we embarked upon what I have since come to regard as an experiment in living.

Because of renovations, our apartment was torn up. There was no kitchen whatsoever, and most of the rest of the apartment was covered in oilcloth. Accordingly, the three of us lived in two back rooms. Our circumstances, coupled with my inadequacy as a parent, brought out Nina and Twig's latent talent for absolute, if subtle, self-aggrandizement. As I tried to perform my duty, they seized every opportunity to fulfill all manner of hitherto undreamed of aspirations. Falling asleep at midnight in front of the television set. Trashing their parents' bedroom. Going for days without a bath. Having Cheerios for dinner. That sort of thing.

School was not yet in session, so they tagged along with me to work, each with a plastic container of dry Cheerios (we had no refrigerator, so milk was out of the question). They proceeded to take over the church offices, attending wedding conferences, terrorizing the staff, sleeping on my office sofa to make up for losses hard-won the night before.

Actually, they were really quite good. That is to say normal, rotten, wonderful kids. Which is one reason single or even primary parenting is so difficult. It's not the things that go wrong that get to you, but the endless repetition and accumulation of everyday things.

I expect, and have observed, that eventually one gets rather good at being a mother. To be fair to myself, three weeks was not a sufficient test. But I did get a taste both of the pain and the reward of daily service in the trenches of parenting. Things like, "You're the best Daddy in the whole wide world," not only abated my temptations to violence, but went a long way toward reminding me of what life is all about.

Today, if I were to be so foolish as to give a sermon on motherhood (or househusbandry), I should choose as my text the Greek myth of Sisyphus.

Every day you roll this stone of yours up to the top of the mountain. Then, just when you reach the top, ready for a well-deserved rest, you lose your grip. Before you can do anything about it, your stone is screaming down the mountainside, bouncing to the bottom once again. Since the stone is your primary responsibility, it doesn't matter how tired you are or how many other things you have to do. You pick your body up, and down you go to fetch your stone, in order to push it up the mountain once again.

You love your stone, of course. And besides, it doesn't know any better than to roll down to the bottom of the mountain every time you get it to the top. Even so, this is a laborious business, certainly not the thing you would prefer to be doing, had you the choice. But you don't have the choice. Paradoxically, even if you did, you would choose to do it just the same.

The original story has no redeeming moral. But when viewed in the light of purgatory, and as a parable for parenting, the myth of Sisyphus reveals the subtle interplay between suffering and salvation. So interpreted, fate is relieved by grace, mottled through and often disguised within an admixture of suffering, sacrifice, and apparent futility. Yet we wouldn't exchange the burden of this responsibility for anything. We may have little to show for a day's worth of pain, but the pain has real meaning, as does any pain that connects us to others.

For pilgrims in purgatory, insights drawn from unaccustomed sources are often among the most illuminating. In her book *In a Different Voice,* Carol Gilligan points out that "in the different voice of women lies the truth of an ethic of care, the tie between relationship and responsibility, and the origins of aggression in the failure of connection."

Purgatory too is defined in terms of a web of interpersonal relationships, rather than by a hierarchy of individual accomplishment. Not that the latter is without pain. The question is simply what such pain means in a world in which God is not so much transcendent as interwoven, a world in which salvation, even survival, is an interdependent, not an independent quest.

The difference between the two models can be summed up simply. Pain in purgatory has meaning, because it connects us to others. Outside purgatory, pain has no meaning beyond itself. Such pain is meaningless, for all pain that does not connect us to another is destined, with its subject, to be lost. As Dorothy Sayers writes in her essay on purgatory, "In Hell, community is lost, or perverted into antagonism; but all Purgatory is united in the bonds of goodwill and of goodwill to earth and Heaven."

In a small town in Israel, a struggling nonsectarian language school suspended classes for three days when a nearby Arab village was flooded by heavy winter rains. The faculty and all the students—Muslims, Christians, and Jews—responded to their neighbors' emergency, working in shifts around the clock to bail the village out. An uncomprehending Israeli minister of education asked the school's director, "What do you think you're doing, when you have your own trouble all around you?" To which she replied, "What's 'around'?"

This is the very nature of the commonwealth of God. When one creature suffers, all suffer with it. Violence here is suicide, freedom responsibility, sacrifice an act of prayer. Again to quote Gilligan,

The concept of identity expands to include the experience of interconnection. The moral domain is similarly enlarged by the inclusion of responsibility and care in relationships. And the underlying epistemology correspondingly shifts from the Greek ideal of knowledge as a correspondence between mind and form to the Biblical conception of knowing as a process of human relationship.

For many of us, our hierarchy of values is based largely on the old competitive ethic of "I win when you lose." That is one reason why virtues still prized and honored so often turn out to be traps. We don't know that we're caught in them, and others by us. The snares of traditional American values—individualistic, tough, gritty, bootstrap values—are deadly, because invisible.

Let's turn to the virtues.

2. Snares of Virtue

The man of superior virtue is not conscious of his virtue,
And in this way he really possesses virtue.
The man of inferior virtue never loses sight of his virtue,
And in this way he loses his virtue.

TAO TE CHING

Be happy. Stay healthy. Feel good. Stay in shape. Treat others like you
want others to treat you. Keep moisturizer on your face.

VANNA WHITE (when asked about her philosophy of life)

If we were to package American virtue in a box we'd have
to put Horatio Alger on the cover. The seven deadly virtues
are bootstrap virtues. In Alger's stories, poor little boys
filled with wile, pluck, and derring-do heroically prove that
virtue is its own reward by employing faith, hope, prudence, temperance, and fortitude in order to clamber over
their more privileged but less driven contemporaries to the
top.

It's hard to insulate oneself against good old Algeresque
virtue. Jesus reigns victorious on television twenty-four hours
a day. The CIA is back in fashion. Latin American drug
barons with impeccable anti-Communist credentials are
subsidized by extortionary arms sales to the Ayatollah. In
Orange County, California, they've even named an airport
after John Wayne.

Not only does virtue seem to insure success—which
to Christians, at least, should be an alien notion—but
success mirrors virtue. Recently, I heard a leading television

evangelist say something like, "This is America. If you're not a winner, it's your own fault." Shortly thereafter I spent a couple of hours chatting on radio with a Christian talk-show host named Bob Larson. In between segments the audience was served up equal portions of antipornography fund appeals and advertisements for "Wee Win Toys." Just imagine:

> Top quality, plush animals like Truthful Teddy, Guardian Angel Bear, Sanctified Skunk, Born Again Bunny . . . [and don't forget the] Action Figures—Moses, John the Baptist, David and Goliath and even Jesus, complete with action casette tapes. Toys of love, toys of adventure, toys to direct young minds toward God.

At the end of the program I mentioned in passing that pornography doesn't exist in the Soviet Union. But let's not get hung up on details. After all, with G.I. Jesus on our side, how can we help but win the battle against evil?

Anyone who extols the entrepreneurial spirit as a virtuistic emblem of the American dream had better include pornographers, pimps, and pushers in the ranks of those who have pulled themselves up by their bootstraps, shown industry and imagination, perceived a want, turned it into a need, and excelled. In fact, if Horatio Alger's hero were growing up today and somehow managed not to end up as a Wall Street insider trader or a Marine lieutenant colonel on special assignment to the White House, you would probably find him on the real streets of America pushing drugs.

Supply side economists are fond of pointing out that a rising tide lifts all the boats. But as the gap grows between rich and poor, which it has every year since 1980, it becomes clear that the rising tide they've been talking about has lifted only the yachts and the battleships; the rowboats got swamped in the wake. It's hardly surprising that a growing number of ambitious young men have chosen to turn in their rowboats for speedboats.

Put yourself in Harlem. Turn on the television for eight or ten years. And then open your door to a pollster who wants you to say a word or two about your philosophy of life. As you look out your window onto 118th Street, is it, "Do unto others as I would have them do unto me" or "Do unto others as they have done unto me by doing for themselves"? Is it America and apple pie, or me and my slice of the American pie?

My guess is that the American dream in Harlem is not all that different from the American dream on campus. When recently asked the same question concerning their philosophy of life, somewhat incongruously a majority of the college students sampled answered, "making money." In fact, since 1967, the ratio of those students who aspire to building a meaningful philosophy of life to those who want to make a lot of money has shifted from 70–30 in favor of philosophy to 70–30 in favor of wealth. I bet it's even true of those who go to church. After all, much religion today has hitched its star to the wagon of success, which carries a load of worldly freight, advertising prosperity to those who believe. The bottom line is the same.

According to the gospel, only one thing distinguishes the pushers and dealers on 118th Street from their light-fingered brothers on Wall Street. For the former the odds are better on making it to the kingdom.

Remember Jesus' parables. Each is designed to shock the smugness out of us: Human laws preempted by divine law; primogeniture cast by the wayside; parties thrown for prodigal children; whores having precedence in the kingdom over moguls. According to Jesus, the bag man in Harlem is greater in the kingdom than the bag man on Wall Street or in Washington.

The reason is simple: He has fewer pretentions to virtue.

We are all insider traders, of course. At one time or another, we have successfully rationalized selling our soul for profit. In our own devious ways, we too have traded weapons for hostages and lied about it, justifying it under another name until everyone was fooled including us. No one is more sincere than a virtuous criminal. After all, there is no shortage of lofty ends to justify whatever means we may chose to elevate our crimes to the status of nobility.

Here, what's good for the goose is also bad for the goose, and may be devastating to the flock. This is true of all the virtues, even temperance. Adolf Hitler was a tee-totaler and a vegetarian. This helped keep his mind and body pure. Hitler was devoted to purity. This same devotion, wildly misunderstood and misapplied, ultimately led him to commit genocide.

Evil is not the privation of good; it is the perversion of good. This is why our "virtues" are so dangerous, both collectively and to us as individuals. Any given quality or value, if lifted above the scale of associated values and weighed independently, becomes an evil.

I think of those people who love humankind; it's just individual human beings they can't stand. Others worship at the altar of freedom at the expense of equity, or the other way around. And then there are those who so love God that they bomb abortion clinics or drive truckloads of dynamite into the embassy of some infidel.

Whenever virtue squeezes out fidelity to the common-weal, we fall victim to idolatry. Apart from community,

righteousness becomes self-righteousness; without responsibility, freedom turns to license. By this measure, patriot-
ism, loyalty, and faith can be the sponsors of fanaticism.
Even love, if not grounded in mutual esteem, soon leads to
possession: possessing our "loved" one as an object, or
being possessed by our passion.

The paradox is that every virtue, when placed on a
pedestal, is potentially deadly, evil veiled beneath its rhetoric and further masked by public applause. To quote St.
John Chrysostom, "Where virtue is, there are many snares."

A snare is something we don't see until we get trapped
in it, but in this case the snares are more subtle. Even after
we get trapped we often don't recognize them. Instead, like
the Pharisee in the gospels, we offer up a prayer to God,
giving thanks that we are pure, "not like other men" (Luke
18:11).

What we need is a taxonomy of deadly virtues.

In her book *Creed or Chaos?*, Dorothy Sayers defines
the seven deadly virtues as "Respectability, Childishness,
Mental Timidity, Dullness, Sentimentality, Censoriousness,
Depression of Spirits." Here, one of the more levelheaded
twentieth-century Christian apologists proves herself to be
a bit of a bluebird. In fact, when ranking virtues according
to toxicity, only one measurement need be taken. As Shakespeare reminds us, "Virtue itself turns vice, being misapplied." Consequently, the deadliness of a virtue when
misapplied is directly proportionate to the honor and esteem in which it is publicly held. *The more elevated the
virtue, the more deadly:* That is the test. By this criterion,
in the above collection of seven deadly virtues, only respectability and sentimentality come close to passing muster.

Even using this simple test to discriminate between

venial and venal virtues (the former being those that have the capacity to poison us only a little), no doubt each of us would figure up a slightly different list. As for myself, being a traditionalist I shall avoid any attempt at originality. Instead of some arbitrary reckoning, I am content to regard the seven traditional Christian virtues as the deadliest virtues of all. Dividing them into their customary groupings, the philosophical virtues (as codified by Plato), and the theological virtues (which were added by Gregory the Great in the sixth century), the seven deadly virtues are as follows: *prudence, justice, temperance, fortitude;* and then, *faith, hope,* and *charity* or *love.*

Over the following pages, I shall ramble among them, discovering ways in which the rhetoric of virtue masks crimes perpetrated in virtue's name, while seeking true virtue in good that is shared, rather than possessed.

As Lao Tse reminds us, there are two types of virtue, the inferior being that which we are most likely to boast of. I call such virtue deadly. This is especially true today, for we have enhanced our powers by attaining knowledge, especially in weaponry, that we lack the wisdom to marshall intelligently. Our world is rife with terrorists for truth and God, inspired by hope, sustained by fortitude, compelled by love, and bereft of wisdom.

In this context, justification by faith alone takes on a different, darker connotation than it did for Martin Luther. In fact, few crimes are potentially more devastating than crimes of ignorance, requiring fortitude and justified by faith, hope, or love.

3. Two Types of Virtue

> The good of the whole is of more account than the good of the part.
>
> ST. THOMAS AQUINAS

> [She] looked towards the window. The dark sky had already paled a little in its frame of cherry-pink chintz. Eternity framed in domesticity. Never mind. One had to frame it in something, to see it at all.
>
> JAN STRUTHER

While lolling about on his veranda late one afternoon, King David caught sight of his beautiful neighbor, Bathsheba, naked in her bath. Greatly enamored, he called her to his bed. Before the evening was over, she was carrying his child.

Recounted in the eleventh chapter of the second book of Samuel, this, one of the great love stories in the Bible, offers a perfect case study for the deadliest virtue of them all.

Upon learning that Bathsheba was pregnant, David recalled her husband, the soldier Uriah, from the field of battle. Were Uriah to lie with his wife quickly, the question of paternity might be blurred. But when Uriah returned, he refused to comply with his sovereign's request, choosing instead to sleep fully armed on David's doorstep.

Frustrated and perplexed, David asked Uriah, who surely must be weary after such a long journey, why he was so stubborn as to resist a bit of refreshment in his own home. "The ark and Israel and Judah dwell in booths," Uriah replied, "and my lord Joab and the servants of my lord are camping in the open field; shall I then go to my house, to eat and to drink, and to lie with my wife? As you live, and as your soul lives, I will not do this thing."

Faced with this testimony of honor, David concocted a second plan to subvert Uriah's will and attain his own end. The next night he got Uriah drunk. But once again, upon suggesting, man to man, that Uriah might enjoy a nightcap with his wife, David was disappointed. The good soldier planted his feet firmly. He held his ground.

With this, David sent Uriah back to the field of battle, carrying a message to Joab. "Set Uriah in the forefront of the hardest fighting, and then draw back from him, that he may be struck down, and die."

And so it came to pass. Bathsheba performed a suitable period of mourning. The two lovers married. And they awaited the birth of their child.

An angry God sent the prophet Nathan, who confronted David with a parable. There were two men, one very poor, the other enormously rich. The poor man owned a single ewe lamb, which he loved as his very daughter, even inviting her to join him and his family at their table. The rich man had more sheep than he could number. One day, having invited a guest to dine with him, the rich man decided to spare his own flock, instead ordering his servants to seize the poor man's lamb, slaughter it, and prepare it for his supper.

As with most parables, Nathan's has two messages, the first obvious and the other veiled. Latching upon the obvious meaning, David expressed his outrage, vowing that the man who committed this unspeakable act deserved to die. To which Nathan responded, "You are the man."

When it comes to recognizing the self-deception of

others, we may sometimes be Nathans, but in the case of our own self-deception, we are almost always Davids. Until Nathan brought the word of God, no one confronted David with his sin because he was king. For us, a veil of virtue serves the same function as David's protective mantle of royalty.

This is no ordinary veil. It has the peculiar property that, when others are unable to see in, we are blocked from seeing out.

David's crime is a crime of love against justice, one virtue against another. But here love is an individual passion, whereas justice is a communal obligation. David's crime is more than a crime against one individual; it is a crime against God.

Yet even purgatory has its heroes, people who against all odds were saved by giving themselves to others, virtuous traitors who entered the fires of heaven and emerged as patriots in the commonwealth of God. One such hero is Ebenezer Scrooge, from Charles Dickens's *A Christmas Carol.*

Scrooge's virtue was prudence. As Pope writes in his *Essay on Man,* "The difference is too nice where ends the virtue or begins the vice." In Scrooge's case, the virtue of prudence was perfected beyond a fare-thee-well. But prudence is where it all began, prudence instructed by hope.

Scrooge's quest was to preserve himself from the soilure of the world. Early in life he put together a formula to insure his freedom from earthly care: Attend to your own business; never meddle in other peoples'; work hard; secure a financial buffer against exigency; avoid sentimental attachments. As he himself put it, "It's enough for a man to understand his own business and not interfere with others."

Scrooge was a model puritan.

Prudence has one primary goal: security. As a shared virtue, few goals are more lofty, but when erected as a bulwark against vulnerability, the fortress of prudence soon becomes a prison. "You fear the world too much," Scrooge's fiancée told him during their parting conversation. "All your other hopes have merged into the hope of being beyond its sordid reproach."

Aptly enough, Scrooge's purgatorial night takes place on Christmas Eve. The story is a familiar one. His old partner Jacob Marley returns from beyond the grave, a ghost "doomed to wander through the world and witness what it cannot share, but might have shared on earth, and turned to happiness." Marley informs Scrooge that he will be visited by three spirits, who turn out to be the ghosts of Christmas past, present, and future. As a gift from his old partner, Scrooge is given the opportunity before he dies to escape from hell, harrow heaven, and enter purgatory.

Not since he was a young man had Scrooge experienced pain. From early on, he had perfected a technique for insulating his life. It was easy, really. Simply avoid the risks that accompany attachment to others. Having been hurt as a child, never would he be hurt again. At least not until that fateful night.

The first spirit tells him, "The memory of what is past makes me hope you will have pain in this." Scrooge begs release. "Spirit," he pleads, "why do you delight to torture me?" Yet, after a night of torment, visited by visions from the past, present, and future (children at play, relatives suffering by virtue of his selfishness, domestic happiness coexisting with poverty and sickness, the jocularity of his business associates upon hearing word of his death, his untended grave), Scrooge is transformed. "I am not the man I was; I will not be the man I must have been except for this."

Few texts better depict the workings of purgatory. Scrooge enters fires that both illumine and purify. He emerges stripped of selfish self-regard and clothed with communal goodwill. For the first time in his life, he celebrates Christmas properly, with lavish gifts, imprudent tips, hearty greetings to strangers, charitable bequests, family celebrations, and generous bonuses. Scrooge abandons the security of his private heaven (which was hell) and enters the commonwealth of God.

So it is that Scrooge escapes the curse of Marley:

"O! captive, bound, and double-ironed," cried the phantom, "not to know that ages of incessant labour, by immortal creatures, for this earth must pass into eternity before the good of which it is susceptible is all developed. Not to know that any Christian spirit working kindly in its little sphere, whatever it may be, will find its mortal life too short for its vast means of usefulness. Not to know that no space of regret can make amends for one life's opportunities misused! Yet such was I! Oh! such was I!"

Such is the nature of purgatory. Darkened by the shadows of death, we perceive the full promise of life. As Robert Browning writes, "Just when we are safest, there's a sunset touch/ A fancy from a flower-bell, someone's death." Each is an emblem of time passing, lending urgency and moment to our days: the sun going down first in glory, then with sweet remembrance; the preciousness that stems from life's fragility; the mortar of mortality that binds us fast to one another.

Life out of death is the quintessential paradox: losing ourselves, we are found; emptying ourselves, we are filled.

The Buddha denies himself Nirvana, instead choosing to share in others' suffering. Christ washes our feet, and dies on a cross.

The secret is to awaken and live before we die, submitting to the pain of illumination, loosing the harness of our self-protective virtues, and running free for others while we can. Our virtues are potentially more deadly than our sins, because they lull us into complacency. Insulated by the feeling that all is right with us, we tend to overlook that all is not right with the world, and that as part of the world, we are part of all that we wrong.

Thornton Wilder's play *Our Town* opens with the burial of Emily Webb, who has died in childbirth during her twenty-sixth year. In the cemetery she recognizes friends and relatives who have died before her, and discovers, as did Marley, that one can return to the land of the living to visit one's past. They advise her not to hazard this, but Emily can't resist. The day she chooses to revisit is her twelfth birthday.

"We'll begin at dawn," the stage manager tells her. "You remember it had been snowing for several days; but it had stopped the night before, and they had begun clearing the roads. The sun's coming up."

"There's Main Street," she says to him. "Why, there's Mr. Morgan's drugstore before he changed it . . . and there's the livery stable . . . Oh, that's the town I knew as a little girl. And look, there's the old white fence that used to be around our house. Oh, I'd forgotten that. I loved it so. Are they inside?" "Yes, your mother'll be coming downstairs in a minute to make breakfast."

As it turns out, Emily's visit is not sweet, for like Marley (who at least could intervene on Scrooge's behalf) she can no longer make a difference in the world, only watch it go by. "I can't go on," she cries to the stage manager. "Oh, it goes so fast. We don't have time to look at one another. I didn't realize. So all that was going on and we never noticed. Take me back—up the hill—to my grave. But first, wait. One more look. Goodbye, world. Goodbye, Grover's Corners. Goodbye, Momma and Papa. Goodbye to clocks ticking . . . and Momma's sunflowers. And food and coffee. And new ironed dresses and hot baths . . . and sleeping and waking up. Do any human beings ever realize life while they are living it—every, every minute."

To which one of her dead companions replies: "Now you know. That's what it was to be alive. To move about in a cloud of ignorance; to go up and down trampling on the feelings of those about you. To spend and waste time as though you had a million years."

What David can't see without Nathan's eyes, Emily only after death, and Scrooge only by observing his life from the grave, is other people, their private pains and struggles, just like our own. In all three cases, overweening self-concern had cast a shadow that obscured the lives of others, even those closest to them. Emily's mother. Tiny Tim. Jim Cratchet. Uriah. In self-deceit, David and Scrooge were true artists, Emily a mere dabbler. But each of them, by withholding it from others, stood squarely in their own light.

Certain feminist and other liberation theologians, forced by the inequity of the old ways to turn ethics inside out, guide us in a different direction. They lead us to an ethic of care based upon relationship rather than self-aggrandizement. How frustrating it must be for them. We continue conducting business in the old way, establishing positions based upon the good of the individual, not the good of society.

This is true of both left and right. One writer compares the ethical positions of two prominent ethicists, John Rawls (a liberal) and Robert Nozick (a conservative), by pointing out that, despite the fact that they reach opposite conclusions on most issues, for both of them:

A society is composed of individuals, each with his or her own interest, who then have to come together and formulate common rules of life.... Individuals are thus in both accounts primary and society secondary, and the identification of individual interests is prior to, and independent of, the construction of any moral or social bonds between them. But ... the notion of desert is at home only in the context of a community whose primary bond is a shared understanding both of the good for man and of the good of that community and where individuals identify their primary interests with reference to those goods.

Our presuppositions are so conditioned by the criteria of individual as opposed to relational virtue, and the logic behind them so well practiced, that it is hard to break through to a new level of discourse. We keep choosing between old, familiar shibboleths, erected on both sides of the ideological fence to protect individual sanctity.

The problem with this sort of thinking is that we are far more intimately related to one another and dependent upon one another than we might imagine. Liberation theologians remind us that when one of God's children suffers, we all suffer. Particle physicists reveal to us the inextricability of forces binding us one to another. Cell biologists alert us to organic macrostructures that incorporate all cellular parts into a living whole.

We have to come to grips with a hard new truth: We belong to one another. This can be understood according to new gathering metaphors in biology and physics. The whole is present in each of the parts, even as each of our cells contains the genetic coding for our whole being. Life is multivalent, with forces and powers inextricably linking all living energy in a complex, dynamic web. From a God's-eye view, not only are we kin to one another, we are part of one another, one body, many members.

To climb the mountain of purgatory, we must open the gates of deadly virtue and pass through them. Until we are able to discriminate between the two types of virtue, this will remain impossible.

There exists no word for virtue in the Jewish scriptures. The closest is *tsedaga,* used in reference to any just or righteous act. Such actions are always contextual. Since they spring from and are judged by the law, they elevate God and the community more than the individual. Such "virtue" is what God expects, having demanded it.

In Greek also, the word often translated justice *(dikaio-sune)* has a corporate, rather than individual connotation. It is what A. W. H. Adkins describes as a "cooperative virtue," as opposed to a competitive one. *Dike,* the word from which it stems, has been defined as "the order of the universe." To be "just" is not to defy that order, even in the name of justice. The one thing that most markedly differentiates the seven deadly virtues from virtue in this larger sense, is their individualistic, and therefore much more easily corrupted, nature.

Throughout history, corporate virtue has been defined in many different ways. In the heroic age of Greece, it was understood in reference to household and community. The word virtue *(arete)* first had the primary connotation of courage or fortitude. But fortitude was not initially an individual virtue, such as might be demonstrated by a boxer or a marathon dancer. It was the hinge upon which the survival of the community turned. As Alasdair MacIntyre writes,

What is alien to our conception of virtue is the intimate connection in heroic society between the concept of courage and its allied virtues on the one hand and the concepts of friendship, fate and death on the other. Courage is important not simply as a quality of individuals, but as the quality necessary to sustain a household and a community.

Over time this connotation expanded, first to include the city-state, as in the Golden Age of Greece; and then, during the Hellenistic and Roman period, to embrace the entire cosmos. According to one philosophical school, the Stoics, virtue is "conformity to cosmic law both in internal disposition and in external act. That law is one and the same for all rational beings; it has nothing to do with local particularity or circumstance."

St. Paul, much influenced by the Stoics, understood this cosmic law in terms of the cosmic Christ. Every member of the church is a member of the body of Christ. Accordingly, individual virtues are always subject to corporate judgment.

When he invokes the image of the body of Christ, Paul asks two things of those whom he invites to participate in it. First he says, "Present your bodies as a living sacrifice, holy and acceptable to God, which is your spiritual worship." Then he says, "Do not be conformed to this world, but be transformed by the renewal of your mind"

(Romans 12:1–5). Each of these requests is an invitation to integrity, (another of those words that suggests wholeness, holiness, and salvation), but the integrity of which he speaks can be understood only in the context of a larger unity, the realm or commonwealth of God.

Paul makes this point most clearly when attempting to reconcile adversaries within the Christian community who differ over the observance of Jewish dietary laws. In Paul's own view, since the earth is the Lord's and the fullness thereof, when it comes to eating, all things are lawful. That which enters our bodies cannot corrupt us, only those things that issue from us, such as cruel words or thoughtless deeds.

Accordingly, Paul divides his Christian brothers and sisters into the strong and the weak. When the strong happen to eat the meat of an animal that has been sacrificed on a pagan altar, they know it can do them no harm. The other Christians are weak. They fear that they may be polluted by such food.

In terms of faith, both groups assign themselves a quotient of virtue, the latter group protecting their faith by abstinence, the former by disregarding such scruples. But Paul doesn't see it that way. Since all virtue is corporate, the good Christian is the one who honors his or her neighbor's scruples, however foolish, and adapts his or her own behavior accordingly.

For Paul the only important thing is that the body of Christ, or the church, not be torn assunder by disputation and rancor. Rather than exhorting his compatriots to demonstrate their fearlessness of "tainted" food in the hopes of converting those whose scruples led them into superstitious error, Paul urged the strong not to offend the weak by eating meat known to have been sacrificed to idols in their presence. "Pursue what makes for peace and for mutual upbuilding," Paul writes in his letter to the Romans. "Do not for the sake of food, destroy the work of God. Everything is indeed clean, but it is wrong for any one to make others fall by what he eats. . . . Let each of us please his neighbor for his good, to edify him" (Romans 14:16–15:2).

This notion is sustained in fits and starts throughout the first Christian centuries all the way to the time of St. Thomas Aquinas. In his *Summa Theologica,* Thomas writes, "The nature of virtue is that it should direct man to good." Here virtue is judged not by its title, but by its fruits.

When virtue directs us to evil rather than good it becomes deadly. Since the rhetoric of virtue is so persuasive, the surest way to protect ourselves against the deadly virtues is by examining those values and principles we most treasure in light of the commonweal. Any virtue worthy of the name builds up others even at our own expense.

Justice calls down judgment; prudence is the ability to discriminate between right and wrong and act accordingly; temperance is self-restraint on behalf of others; fortitude is the courage to suffer for another; faith is the confidence that life has meanings we shall never finally know or be able to name; hope is the expectation that salvation, shared health and wholeness, remains possible.

As for love, it is our mutual devotion to goods, whether material or spiritual, that can only be held in common. Which is why, as Paul said, "Love does not insist upon its own way" (1 Corinthians 13), and why, when it does so insist, as with every virtue, love is deadly—in direct proportion to the elevation of its object.

At the end of Umberto Ecco's novel *The Name of the Rose,* the greatest library in Christendom burns to the ground, torched by a monk. The "holy" man's zeal for Christ leads him to hide and finally to destroy any evidences that might inspire sophisticated Christians to waver in their belief. As Ecco's protagonist, William of Baskerville, explains to his young disciple, Adso:

> The Antichrist can be born from piety itself, from excessive love of God or of the truth, as the heretic is born from the saint and the possessed from the seer. Fear prophets, Adso, and those prepared to die for the truth, for as a rule they make many others die with them, often before them, at times instead of them. Jorge did a diabolical thing because he loved his truth so lewdly that he dared anything in order to destroy falsehood.

William of Baskerville is a great medieval sleuth, pre-cursor of Sherlock Holmes. Here he not only solved a crime (the series of murders leading up to the final conflagration), but also uncovered the motive for them.

In most cases, crimes of virtue prove difficult to solve, in part because they remain undetected and in part because they are committed unwittingly. Even as the devil is "evil disguised as good," criminals who invoke the seven deadly virtues trade in deceit. And as often as not—as with David, Scrooge, and Emily—the first people we manage to deceive are ourselves.

Our sins will be forgiven, of course. But only when we recognize that we have sinned do we know enough to ask for forgiveness. This is one of the reasons why our virtues are more deadly than our sins. And not only to us.

As Ecco himself puts it, "Because of excess virtue the forces of hell prevail."

4. Virtue *Über Alles*

Every institution finally perishes by an excess of its own basic principle.
LORD ACTON

Fogarty, the only thing worse than spying for the Russians is telling your own people the truth.
MARK JOSEPH, *To Kill the Potemkin*

You may be interested to know that the wolves have a different version of Little Red Riding Hood than we do. It's not all that surprising really. The meaning of a story and even its details change according to the perspective of the one who is telling it. This is true of everything from Custer's Last Stand to the four holy gospels. In any event, as a scholar might phrase it, here is the lupine redaction of the Riding Hood tale:

Once upon a time there was a good wolf, always helpful to others, always kind. One day, when walking through the woods on his morning constitutional, he encountered a little girl dressed all in red. At first he was frightened, because humans have a history of being cruel to wolves, but he overcame his fear and welcomed her to his part of the woods.

"Where are you going, little girl?" the kind wolf asked. "To my grandmother's house on the other side of the forest," the little girl replied. "My grandmother is very old and very ill, and I am taking her this picnic basket filled with treats to make her young and well again."

What a sweet little girl, thought the wolf to himself, yet

so naive, so unschooled in the ways of the woods, which are the ways of life and death. The more he pondered this, the more worried he became. Perhaps he should have accompanied the little girl, not just to protect her from any who might wish her harm, but also gently to share with her a little of his wisdom, lest, as children often do, she should end up feeling in some way responsible when her grandmother died.

By this time the little girl had quite a head start. Nonetheless, the good wolf put down his walking stick and ran as fast as he could to the little girl's grandmother's house, taking a shortcut he knew, hoping perhaps to accompany the little girl home, during which time they could discuss these things at leisure.

When he arrived at the grandmother's house, the wolf knocked on her door, unsure as to whether or not the little girl had already arrived. There was no answer. He knocked again. Still no answer. The door was unlatched so he entered the cottage, only to discover the little girl's grandmother lying lifeless in her bed. She had no pulse and was not breathing. Desperately, he attempted artificial respiration, but to no avail. He could not resuscitate her.

Just then he heard the little girl singing sweetly in the distance as she approached the cottage. Determined to protect her from the shock of finding her grandmother dead, he had to think fast. Then it struck him. He had one chance, albeit a risky one. Though he had already enjoyed a good breakfast and was not hungry at all, he wolfed the old woman down, threw on her nightgown, and jumped under the covers.

Despite the wolf's best intentions, as so often happens everything went wrong that possibly could. To begin with, his disguise was far from perfect. When the little girl came in, her curiosity concerning her grandmother's appearance led her to ask a number of questions, about the length of her nose, for instance, and the depth of her voice, but when she commented upon the size of her grandmother's teeth and the wolf replied as sweetly as possible, "The better to eat with, my dear" (prejudice later added the "you"), the little girl recognized that this was not her grandmother at all, screamed, and ran from the cottage. The good wolf pursued her, trying to explain, but before he had the chance, a hunter leapt from the underbrush and shot him dead.

Very sad.

Wolves love to hear this story, I am told. Around the den at nighttime, when Daddy and Mommy tuck the cubs into bed, it is the one they usually ask to hear, even though they know it by heart. The moral never fails to move them. Even though the good wolf was killed, in a way he died for all wolves, for through the example of his life generations of wolves have been inspired to perform unself-regarding deeds of kindness.

Critics within the wolf community say this smacks of self-deception, but surely the tellers of tales can be forgiven for stretching the truth in their favor. After all, it's only human. There are always at least two sides to every story. The trouble really begins when these two sides, either literally or figuratively, are lined up against one another on a field of battle. Between the trenches the rhetoric of good versus evil is mirrored, one side's good being evil to the other, and vice versa. This might prove bewildering to an impartial observer, but there are no impartial observers.

Recently a number of studies have been done on the ways in which we caricature our enemies. By comparing political propaganda (patriotic cartoons, posters, etc.) from opposing countries during a time of war, students of patriotic hatred have convincingly displayed the parallels: Grotesque images mock one another, opposing leaders—ours and theirs—defaced with the visage of pigs, dogs, or skulls, each representation designed to dehumanize the enemy.

Sometimes the enemy is as evil as our representations make him or her out to be. Certainly this was true of Adolf Hitler. As sponsor of the holocaust, a case study in evil disguised as good, here was a man more satanic than the most vicious caricature could ever portray. Yet, ironically, as Kurt Vonnegut, Jr., points out, "This was very bad for us. . . . Our enemies were so awful, so evil, that we, by contrast, must be remarkably pure. That illusion of purity, to which we were entitled in a way, has become our curse today."

He is absolutely right. Since all of us are impure, the most dangerous self-definition is the negative-print image, as drawn from the portraits we manufacture of our enemies, whether they are accurate or not. The proof goes as follows. "Our enemies are evil. We are against them. Therefore we are good."

Both sides can play this game, and almost always do. There is more than enough evil in the world to give both "us" and "them" incentive to mount crusades to vanquish whatever evil we perceive in the actions or systems of the other. By definition, such an end is so noble that the means almost always become secondary. In the names of freedom, justice, and truth, both we and they end up fighting crime by criminal means, and delinquency by becoming delinquents.

Consider a little-known episode in American history, the debate over amnesty in 1783–84. The controversy began with the publication of the Preliminary Articles of Peace, drafted in Paris in 1783 and sent to the Continental Congress for preliminary approval. One of these was a recommendation that the states permit Loyalists to return for the purpose of negotiating the restitution of their property and lands. In the language of the Fifth Article, Benjamin Franklin and John Jay, the American negotiators, proposed that such a gesture conformed with "that spirit of conciliation, which, on the return of the blessing of peace, should universally prevail."

Initially, few others agreed. The papers were peppered with derisive editorial notices: "Here you cannot live," the Tories were told. "Your friends cannot help you. A cold congressional recommendation cannot save you. You shewed no mercy to your country and you will have judgment without mercy. . . . Justice forbids any compensation or favor to Tories."

Then, as today, to many Americans a nation "under God" should act in conformity to the will of God. The problem with such a standard is that in setting public policy "God's will" may be shaped to conform to our own desires. Several more recent examples suggest themselves, but before considering one of them, let's take a closer look at this earlier debate, a perfect case study in the ambiguities implicit in the rhetoric of virtue.

The most memorable sermon devoted to the opponents' cause was Nathaniel Whitaker's "The Reward of Toryism." A Salem minister and thoroughgoing Calvinist, Whitaker found mercy to be entirely inappropriate to the vigorous prosecution of God's righteous judgment. "Love, forgiveness of enemies, and compassion, are most amiable virtues," he wrote, "but they degenerate into criminal weakness, as they spring from a vitiated heart." Whitaker's text was Joshua 7:13: "There is an accursed thing in the midst of thee, O Israel; thou canst not stand before thine enemies, until ye take away the accursed thing from among you."

One problem with the Bible as a proof-text for the interpretation of virtue is that the same verse can be invoked by opposing sides. To Charles Chauncy, a minister from Boston with strong Universalist leanings, the accursed thing was "impiety towards God, unrighteousness and unmercifulness towards our neighbor." But to Whitaker, it was the Tories. "The curse required is a serious, deliberate, religious act of justice, which God requires of us."

Claiming that as a Christian he was answerable only to God and not to members of Congress, Whitaker flatly pronounced that he would never comply with their recommendation. He urged his listeners to wash their hands of it entirely or to suffer the consequences.

If the argument from justice found its most eloquent advocate in Whitaker, that of mercy was as staunchly represented by John Lathrop of the Second Church in Boston. To a Universalist such a Lathrop, God was a merciful, all-forgiving God. In his ordination sermon for William Bentley in 1783, using as his text Titus 2:11, he declared that "the grace of God *bringeth salvation to all men.* Wherever the gospel is preached, salvation is proclaimed to guilty cratures." Offering the most perfect model for this, Jesus "sent his apostles to proclaim the gospel of divine grace *to every creature,* urging them to repent of their sins, and promising them happiness in proportion to the improvement they should make of their talents and advantages, under a most gracious dispensation."

The Fifth Article of Peace was finally ratified. Time healed old wounds, amnesty was granted to the Tories, and all the glorious rhetoric turned to dust, with the exception of a few words sufficiently humble to be worth remembering. "If I err," John Lathrop said, "it is on the side of mercy; and you will all say, to err on this side, is more excusable in a minister of Jesus Christ, a great part of whose business it is to proclaim the forgiving mercy of God, than to err on the side of justice."

Religion is defined only in a handful of places in the Bible, with Micah's definition perhaps the most inclusive: "And what does the Lord require of you," he asks, "but to do justice, love mercy, and walk humbly with your God." When the first two injunctions are in conflict, the third becomes essential.

Militant ethics based upon God's justice or even God's love, when advocated with pride and not humility, are, by Micah's definition, impious. They mask their own crime, which is a crime against the very virtue they pronounce. For instance, love of one country often expresses itself as fear of another, and fear leads us to hate. Even if the system we oppose is hateful, actions instructed by fear are likely to be more consonant with a hateful system of government than a loving one. Here another of Micah's admonitions— "The best of us is like a briar; the most upright of us a thorn hedge . . . Our confusion is at hand"—becomes not only figuratively but also literally true.

If, answering to a "higher call," Nathanial Whitaker attempted to subvert the will of a "misguided Congress" in order that justice might be done, similar confusions of virtue have occurred in our own time, putting Seneca's adage that "Virtue with some is nothing but successful temerity" to the test, and finding it not wanting.

A little background.

In 1976, the bicentennial year of the Declaration of Independence, my father, Frank Church, chaired the Senate Select Committee on Intelligence. He was charged with the task of investigating assassination plots against foreign leaders, and other possible crimes committed by agencies of the U.S. government under the cloak of covert action. During the course of that investigation, in an interview with *Parade Magazine,* he recalled that

> George Williams, one of the much-beloved professors of theology at Harvard Divinity School, once said to me something that I have always remembered. "Choose your enemy very carefully, for you will grow to be more like him." After World War II the Soviet Union became our perceived enemy and we undertook to contest with the Russians everything in the world. To justify emulating their method we said we had to treat fire with fire. And in the process, of course, we've become more like them. . . . We've become our own worst enemy.

Thirteen years later, in the 1987 Iran-Contra hearings, a lieutenent colonel of the United States Marine Corps invoked "the love of God and the love of this nation" in defending his own actions as implementer of a bizarre series of covert actions that skirted if not broke the law, and did considerable damage to our nation's integrity.

Rarely have the seven deadly virtues had a better showcase than during the testimony of Colonel Oliver North. His motives were lofty ("I want you to know lying does not come easy to me, . . . but I think we all had to weigh in the balance the difference between lives and lies"); his cause noble ("The Nicaraguan freedom fighters [unlike the Sandanistas?] are people—living, breathing, young men and women"); and his conscience clear ("I am going to walk from here with my head high and my shoulders straight because I am proud of what we accomplished. I am proud of the efforts that we made, and I am proud of the fight that we fought").

In its protestation of innocence, North's testimony leaves one nostalgic for lost guilt. Not only that, but he played to a packed and cheering house of Americans. "Providence told Ollie North to take Capitol Hill," wrote theologian Michael Novak; "North for President" billboards sprang up like weeds; tens of thousands of telegrams favorable to North flooded Washington; sympathetic senators lauded him as an American hero, "a dedicated, patriotic soldier, and there's no question you've gone above and beyond—on many occasions—the call of duty."

Indeed.

Here we have the perfect recipe for deadly virtue: Take any set of actions, however half-baked or rancid, dress them with a liberal helping of God and family, add a bit of individual spiciness, wrap the whole dish in the American flag, and give it a name like "Project Democracy."

Psychiatrist Robert Coles credited North's remarkable public appeal to old-fashioned American values. People saw him as

the head of a two-parent family, "a solid and normal one," as one mother said, commenting not only on the colonel, but his wife, too—her appearance, her choice of clothes, her manner of response to her husband. It was as if Norman Rockwell's 1940s gauzy American romanticism had suddenly found an incarnation, hence a moment of redemption. Someone, someplace still lives the old-fashioned virtuous life—fights in a war bravely, comes home with medals, is a good husband and father, is religious, takes it on the chin and suffers with dignity while others walk away discreetly, someone who has regrets for not being with his family more, yet is an adventurer, even a bit of a rogue, but all for the beloved nation.

Not everyone bought Oliver North's testimony. Many commentators in the press and several members of the Joint Committee eloquently spoke of their concern. Senator Paul Sarbanes expressed his dismay by quoting Justice Brandeis: "The greatest dangers to liberty lurk in insidious encroachments, by men of zeal, well meaning, but without understanding." And Chairman Daniel Inouye, himself a much-decorated war hero who lost his arm in World War II, echoed the words of my father, asking rhetorically, "should we in the defense of democracy, adopt and embrace one of the most important tenets of communism and Marxism— the ends justify the means?"

As Colonel North's testimony shows, we can so love our country that we are willing to destroy the principles upon which it is founded.

Since these days that may only be the beginning, perhaps we ought to start over again.

5. Playing with Fire

As far as I could see, the will of God was simply that everything possible would indeed be possible. Within that limitation the choice was ours, the reckoning God's. And God was in us, that was the Fire of it, that was the Garden of it, at the center of every soul and contiguous with infinity.

RUSSELL HOBAN

Once upon a time a man and woman lived together in a garden. It was paradise: fruit-bearing trees in abundance, perfect weather, nothing to do but frolic naked without shame, perhaps bathe in the bubbling brook, or loll in the shade, naming an occasional animal. No appointments to keep, no tasks to fulfill, no bodily pains, no fear of death for there was no death, not even any rules, save one: God forbade the man and woman from eating fruit from the tree of the knowledge of good and evil.

One day a serpent sidled up to the woman. "Eve," he said, "you're being foolish. God told you to keep clear of that tree, because the old scoundrel wants to make sure that you never grow up. It's a paternalistic power play. The moment you bite into that fruit your eyes shall be opened; you too shall be God's equal, blessed with the knowledge of good and evil."

Persuaded by the serpent, Eve talked to Adam and they decided to give knowledge a try. It turned out the serpent had spoken truth, but not the whole truth. As promised, they became as gods, knowing good and evil. But God tucked away a wild card. When Adam and Eve drew knowledge, God trumped it with death.

Immortality and the powers of judgment are two main-stays of divinity. As the record shows, before the fall we were godlike in immortality, but not in knowledge. This Adam and Eve purchased at the price of death, inheriting the burdens of a hard, brief existence. Adam was to sweat among the thorns and thistles of the field, Eve to labor in delivering of children. Both were sentenced to return at the end of their days to the dust from which they came (Genesis 1–2).

As with all stories, this tale of birth and fate may be read in different ways. One of the most intriguing readings springs from the mystical well of certain Gnostics, those Jewish and later Christian sectarians who founded their religion not on law or faith, but on knowledge *(gnosis)*. This particular group of Gnostics went by the name Sethi-ans. They worshiped the snake.

Think about it.

If you considered knowledge the most prized of all possessions, how would you regard a God who conspired to prevent you from winning this prize? Not with reverence, surely. And what about the agent who offered you the key to knowledge?" Try "my strength and my redeemer."

Not unlike the Moslems, who trace the divine inheri-tance from Ishmael instead of Isaac, the Sethians took Genesis and turned it on its head, claiming that a higher God sent the serpent into Eden to liberate Adam and Eve from thralldom. *Felix culpa* (blessed sin), as medieval the-ologians used to say, given that without the fall poor Jesus couldn't die to save us. In this case, the fall is redemptive in its own right, bringing with it the first major advance in human intelligence. By eating from the tree of knowledge, we tasted the fruit of the gods.

However one chooses to interpret the first two chapters of Genesis, the fruit from the tree of knowledge of good and evil constitutes a powerful metaphor. We have spent millennia just beginning to digest it. As its juices work their way through our system we change, becoming ever more awesome in our powers. Today we possess both the powers of creation (with the splicing of genes) and the powers of destruction (with the splitting of atoms). From Genesis to Revelation, from the alpha of creation to the omega of apocalypse, God's domain has become our own.

When Neil Armstrong, an American earthling, walked on the moon, the Islamic peoples were scandalized. The moon had been desecrated; there would be hell to pay. I was working that summer in Washington, D.C., as a groundskeeper for the Park Service, tending the earth and keeping it in a modest sort of way. The moonwalk scandalized my coworkers for a different reason. They didn't believe it had happened, not really. A Hollywood production, they said, whipped up to take people's minds off of real problems—racism, the plight of the poor—our own modern proof in point of Marx's like characterization of religion as the opiate of the masses.

Other religious overtones spring to mind: the astronauts' reading of Genesis 1, broadcast back to earth from the spacecraft on its return flight from the heavens.

Then God said, "Let us make humankind in our image, after our likeness; and let them have dominion over the fish of the sea, and over the birds of the air, and over the cattle, and over all the earth . . . "So God created humankind in God's own image . . . male and female . . . And God blessed them, and said to them, "Be fruitful and multiply and fill the earth and subdue it."

From today's perspective these are ominous words, words in stark contrast to those of the Psalmist—"The earth is the Lord's and the fullness thereof"—recast by Paul in his attempt to reconcile conflicting members of the body of Christ (Romans 14:8). Such dominion gives a haunting turn to the most telling phrase in the inaugural address of the president who, before being martyred, led us into space. "Here on earth," John F. Kennedy said, "God's work must truly be our own."

Think of the new technologies and the questions they raise, from Baby Doe to Baby M, from Hiroshima to Armageddon. With our knowledge continuing to outstrip our wisdom, whether we can handle God's work remains highly doubtful. But if not, there *will* be hell to pay, since the punishment for *hubris,* the usurpation of powers belonging to the gods by human beings who have no natural right to them, is *nemesis,* utter and terrible destruction.

Two other legends have a bearing here, the tales of Prometheus and Faust. Running parallel to the first chapters of Genesis, the tale of Prometheus goes as follows: Zeus made humankind out of clay. At first, relegated to a station little higher than the beasts, lacking all knowledge of the heavenly secrets and possessing only the most rudimentary tools, we posed no threat to him. But then Prometheus, half-god half-man, stole fire from heaven, empowering us with new technology that lifted us beyond our bestial state. Zeus punished Prometheus by chaining him to a mountain crag, where an eagle daily fed on his liver, which was restored each succeeding night. But meanwhile, with the gift of fire and other godlike powers of craft and art brought down from Olympus, Prometheus succeeded in liberating the human race from bondage to Zeus.

Contrast this with the tale of Dr. Faustus, the sixteenth-century German magician who, in exchange for knowledge and power, sold his soul to the devil. At first he was depicted as little more than a fool (in the original puppet plays) or charlatan (in Christopher Marlowe's *Doctor Faustus*). But over the years the Faust legend underwent a telling metamorphosis. Throughout the Age of Reason, as our faith in science and technology grew, people began to see Faust's crime in a new light. This, coupled in the nineteenth century with the romantic lionization of superheroes, men and women who dared to flout convention, led to the resurrection of Faust as a modern hero, a natural protagonist. First Lessing and then Goethe rewrote the Faust legend with a happy ending. Individual human genius augmented by power proves stronger than the devil. Faust wins his wager and is saved.

But then follows our century: two world wars, the Holocaust, the atomic bomb. Destruction reigned as never before, translating from triumphant to tragic Faust's imperious individualism. Thomas Mann in his novel *Doctor Faustus*, written just after the Second World War, suggests that neither Lessing's principle of education nor Goethe's Hegelian synthesis is sufficient to rescue Faust from this new hell. Following in lockstep with the ravaging of Europe, tragic, brilliant, modern Dr. Faustus, feverishly burning, reaps what he and his century have sown.

Prometheus and Faust both seek powers hitherto denied to humankind, and both suffer as a result. But where Prometheus's suffering has meaning, Faust's does not. Dr. Faust sells his soul to the devil for his own selfish purposes. A modern-day gnostic, he seeks knowledge and mastery for their own sake, regardless of the consequences.

On the other hand, Prometheus, in jeopardizing his future, does so not for himself but explicitly to guarantee a better future for humankind. Each is playing with fire, for one the fire of hell, for the other the fire of heaven. In wresting control of divine powers that enhance our status in the great chain of being, what Faust receives from the devil, Prometheus takes from God.

Knowledge is not virtue, it is power, and power can be employed for good or evil. The fires of knowledge can either purify or incinerate, depending upon whether or not they burn away the trappings of self-aggrandizement. In the ancient and medieval world, as Alasdair MacIntyre writes, the egoist is "always someone who has made a fundamental mistake about where his own good lies and someone who has thus and to that extent excluded himself from human relationship." MacIntyre contrasts this with Aristotle's view of cooperative, rather than competitive virtue, in which our good as individuals is one with the good of those others with whom we are related in human community. We cannot pursue our own good in a way necessarily antagonistic to others pursuing theirs because the good belongs not to either of us alone but to both of us together. "Goods are not private property," he concludes.

Indeed. They are exclusive possessions of the commonweal.

This is not an argument in favor of collectivism. In both its arcadian and utopian forms, collectivism is nothing more than corporate individualism: Everyone acts alike, not together. As reflected in the distinctiveness of members of the body of Christ, the commonwealth of God is based upon mutuality, not conformity. Diversity is not only permitted here; it is honored. But never at the expense of the commonweal.

Martin Buber told the story of modern history by reminding his listeners that constitutional government was originally founded upon three principles: liberty, equality, and fraternity. Over the years liberty traveled west to be enshrined in capitalism; equality gravitated east and became the linchpin of communism. In each instance, fraternity got lost. Buber called fraternity (the kinship of all people) the spiritual principle.

To redress the balance, as Christopher Lasch writes,

We need a conception of politics that is neither communitarian nor individualistic, a conception best described as fraternal. Fraternity recognizes the boundary between the self and others. It does not try to annihilate the self in order to bring about a condition of universal brotherhood. But this doesn't rule out the hope of a common life. On the contrary, a politics based on fraternity is the only thing that makes a common life possible, because it creates the possibility of trust.

In contrast, any individual—or nation for that matter—who builds himself up at the expense of others, scoring victories, adding notches to his gun, is lighting the fuse for his or her own self-destruction.

Competitive virtues elevate winners by diminishing losers. In the age of the global village and the global economy, this is especially hazardous in competition between countries. Although the balance may be tipped temporarily in one side's favor, if sustained such imbalances set up the possibility of a *tsunami,* a tidal wave of terrifying proportion that may start on one side of the world and end up crashing down on the other.

Given human nature and history, to propose a relational, cooperative, fraternal or kinship-based ethic fashioned to strengthen the interdependent web of being may seem idealistic and naive. In fact, it is desperately realistic. As we have learned from the global stock market crash of October 1987, interrelatedness is not simply a theological concept; it is a new truth. In economics, protectionism no longer protects. In nuclear warfare, superiority no longer offers advantage. Cast in their competitive, individualistic form, the old virtues are deadly, our hope hopeless, our faith groundless. With the advent of global communications, multinational commerce, and nuclear weaponry, we live in a new and different world. No longer are we made secure by our own security; we are made insecure by others' insecurity.

The problem is that our privatistic virtues and competitive habits are so ingrained, the institutions that support them so well established, and our status outside the commonwealth of God so beguiling, that the same realism which commends purgation of the old ways and the kindling of new argues against our risking the pain. After all, we are accustomed to our comfortable arguments and old enemies.

Not only that, but, when it comes to spiritual purgation, the fires of the Gods burn, offering incentive to avoid them. In the words of an anonymous prayer rich in purgatorial allusion:

> Self-deceit is a strong fort;
> It will last a lifetime.
> Self-truth is a lightning bolt lost as I grasp it.
> And the fires that it strikes can raze my house.
> You ask me to yearn after truth, God.
> But who would choose to be whipped with fire?
> Unless the lightning that strikes terror
> Lights enough to show the boundaries

Where terror ends,
And at the limits, still enduring and alive,
Shows me myself
And a hope no longer blind.

Blind hope too is a deadly virtue. It anchors modern-day idealism, if by this we mean a belief in chimeras, the stuff out of which dreams spin trillion-dollar budgets for star-wars technology to protect us against our own inventions.

When Aeschylus wrote *Prometheus Bound,* even when Marlowe wrote his *Doctor Faustus,* our world was a divided world—the heavens above, the earth below. We were the center of the universe, of God's attention, yet ever in danger of becoming estranged from God by thinking too much of ourselves. The old pattern of hubris and nemesis, presumption and fall, was understood in the context of a divided ground of spiritual being, ours and God's. Unsolicited trespass beyond our appointed territory invited swift destruction.

Two major shifts decisively alter our perspective. First, we are no longer the center of the universe. Not only does the sun not revolve around the earth, but the sun itself is a lesser sun in the great scheme of things, a peripheral star.

The other shift is that, even as we recognize ourselves to have receded in cosmic importance, we continue to augment our human powers to such an extent that powers once considered the unique prerogative of God, the powers of creation and apocalypse, are within our human grasp. We are no longer only responsible for our own salvation, but for the cultivation and preservation of life itself. It is not so much that we have arrogated God's prerogative; rather we have inherited certain essential responsibilities once thought to be exclusively a part of the heavenly domain. With reverence and humility, we must employ our new technologies to human ends, lest demons of our own devising run amok and destroy their creators in an unthinkable apocalypse.

Upon tasting the fruit of knowledge, we inherited the responsibility of the gods, to choose between good and evil. Not having fully digested this fruit, such choices are hard. And we are not skilled in making them. Yet the moment we are liberated from choosing, we shall be stripped of our humanity, and with this, of our hope for reunion with God.

What is called for is a new spiritual consciousness of our interdependencies, upon one another and between ourselves and all that lives and sustains life on earth. Should a new religious model be required, its nature is suggested by that stunning image of the blue-green earth as seen from space, marbled with white clouds, rising over the moon's horizon. "Think of how we spoke of things under the old model," Joseph Campbell reminds us:

Everything was seen from earthbound eyes. The sun rose and set. Joshua stopped both the sun and the moon to have time to finish a slaughter. With the moonwalk, the religious myth that sustained these notions could no longer be held. With our view of earthrise, we could see that the earth and the heavens were no longer divided but that the earth is in the heavens . . . There is a unity in the universe.

In the first chapter of Genesis, humankind was created in the image of God. We were given dominion over the earth, charged to fill the earth and to subdue it. But in the second chapter, which reflects a different strand of the ancient traditions brought together in the Bible, we are placed here not to subdue the earth, but "to dress and to keep it."

Given the knowledge of good and evil, if like Faust we continue to use that knowledge for selfish, shortsighted, and narrow purposes, our hubris will surely lead to a nemesis of ultimate proportions. But if, like Prometheus, we share our warmth and light, then the fires we empowered to kindle will burn to bless and keep our world like beacons of true hope, guiding our fellow travelers through the dark yet luminous purgatorial night.

6. Chariots of Fire

Those times—those last days of earth! I think about them a lot ... There were so many religions in conflict, each ready to save the world with its own dogma, each perfectly intolerant of the other. Every day seemed a mere skirmish in the long holy war. It was a time of debauch and conversion.

E. B. WHITE

I came to cast fire upon the earth; and would that it were already kindled.

JESUS (LUKE 12:49)

I wonder if this is how the world will end. On one side, maybe ours, a computer error. Scrambled signals in the data feed. Orders misdirected. Backup computers fail. Who knows what might happen to pull us off course without our knowing it?

After all, our crews are highly trained. Our systems are the best. As far as anyone can tell, everything's in order except, perhaps, the communications system. For some odd reason those in charge, some second-level commander and his crew, can't seem to communicate with anyone. Nothing much to worry about. They tinker a bit, chatting among themselves about the folks back home. I wonder. Could the beginning of the end of the world be anything like this? A computer failure? An innocent mistake?

On the other side, maybe theirs, an alarm sounds. Something is amiss. Systems are readied and placed on full alert. Interceptors are sent out. Those in charge, some second-level commander and his crew, try to communicate with us, but only briefly, and their attempts at communication fail. They perceive intent instead of error in our actions, mistaking us for something we are not. Or perhaps they simply go by the book: Act first and ask questions later, just as they have been instructed to do. A deadly mistake. They open fire.

And what about the rest of us, passengers on a voyage through space, friend and foe alike, Christian, Moslem, Jew, Buddhist, Hindu, black and white, Communist and capitalist, traveling in enforced togetherness toward a common destiny?

We are flying through the night. The shades are drawn, the lights low. One woman gently rocks her baby, another puts the final touches on a major article that she hopes may revolutionize her field. Some of us are drinking, some conversing quietly with friends. One young man plays solitaire, another studies for his exams. Many are tucked in for the evening, wrapped in blankets, fitfully dreaming or sleeping soundly.

Or are we all nodding, fitfully or soundly, half-asleep to the dangers that, without warning, threaten to terminate the fragile experiment of life upon this planet?

It is hard to imagine as we make our plans for tomorrow. And love our children. And hate our enemies. And build up our arsenals, both personal and national, to defend ourselves against them. It is hard to imagine as we doze off with our tickets in our pockets. First an innocent mistake, then a deadly mistake. And no one left to report that the target has been destroyed.

This is the only difference: The confusion, countercharges, and denials offered by both sides following the downing of Korean airliner 007 by Soviet jets over the sea of Japan in 1983 would not follow the destruction of the earth in a nuclear holocaust.

Nothing would.

In *Blessed Assurance,* A. G. Mojtabai's study of the relationship between the nuclear arms industry in Amarillo, Texas, and the theology of the new Religious Right, she suggests that what is missing in this theology is the vision of community, here and now on earth, a shared humanity in which all God's children must find their way haltingly, but hand in hand, toward peace. Instead, what we get is a vision of community—all God's children living together in harmony—*after* the rapture. The fire of judgment burns, winnowing out the chaff in apocalyptic furnaces, and all those sealed in Christ arise and enter the gates of the kingdom. Since Armageddon is the hinge upon which redemption finally turns, the nuclear arms race appears to certain born-again Christians in a somewhat different light than it does for the rest of us.

As the President of the United States said to an Israeli lobbyist in 1983, "You know, I turn back to your ancient prophets in the Old Testament and the signs foretelling Armageddon, and I find myself wondering if—if we're the generation that's going to see that come about. I don't know if you've noted any of these prophecies lately, but believe me, they certainly describe the times we're going through." In such expressions as this, faith may surpass love as the deadliest virtue of all.

Plato tells the story of a charioteer and his two fiery steeds. One day when driving, the charioteer grows drowsy and drifts off to sleep. No longer feeling the restraint of the reins, his steeds bolt from their path, leading both themselves and their driver in uncontrolled flight toward the abyss.

In this story, the driver is drawn into danger unconscious of his peril. But as the chariot lurches toward the pit, a distant bystander, perceiving the danger, issues an alarm. In a ringing voice, he shouts out to the charioteer, "Wake up! Save yourself!" The startled driver awakens, perceives his peril, draws in his steeds, and saves himself from certain destruction.

Plato interprets this parable in terms of self-discipline rather than relationship. The two fiery steeds are intended to represent animal desires, lusts, and passions, which, when uncontrolled, can dominate our individual lives and even destroy them. The driver is the understanding, the intelligence, the wisdom we are endowed with that we might tame our desires and have dominion over our impulses.

There is a modern way to read this parable. From the standpoint of knowing relationships rather than self-knowledge, salvation entails community, not individual, effort. It has communal as well as individual consequences. By such a reading, the key moment in this story comes when a distant bystander bestirs himself and issues a call of alarm.

Adapted to contemporary realities, we might interpret Plato's parable as follows:

This is a nuclear chariot. The fiery steeds represent "hope" and "fortitude," to which the driver has given increasingly loose rein. Our hope lies in the continuing power of deterence. Our fortitude rests in the will never to stint in amassing armaments to protect ourselves from, even ultimately to vanquish, an evil, Godless adversary. These arguments have been offered up so often, and with such persuasive passion, that the driver of this deadly cargo has been lulled asleep. Thus, when the distant bystander cries out, not only is he protecting the charioteer from self-destruction, but also himself and his neighbors from being immolated when the chariot, a potential fireball of unprecedented proportion, careens into the abyss towards which it is hurtling.

In Plato's reading, an individual is saved from his personal passions, which we later called sins. Today, what threatens the survival of one individual endangers us all— not our sins so much as our "virtues," our ideological passions, things in which we have absolute faith, insured by hope and defended by fortitude. We employ these "virtues" to legitimate our power, sharpen our competitive edge, establish criteria of superiority, and defend otherwise indefensible actions. In an age in which survival itself hinges upon the development of an alternative set of relational values, the old virtues, practiced in the old ways, are deadly.

This is true both of nation states and individuals. There is no virtue that cannot lead us down the time-honored path to the deadliest of the seven deadly sins, the sin of pride. "Our virtues are most frequently but vices in disguise," wrote La Rochefoucauld in his maxims. Stemming from the Latin root *vir*, or "man," our virtues, when untempered by humility, more often prove our manliness than they do our humanity.

This is not merely a theological point; it is a matter of immediate practical concern. Today, for the first time in history, we earthlings are fully capable of producing hellfire in sufficient quantity to stage Armageddon all by ourselves. Our only hope lies with the commonwealth of God. Perhaps the fires of purgatory, heaven-sent to purify us of our deadly virtues, can save us from the fires of hell which, in the case of nuclear holocaust, would incinerate us on virtue's behalf.

Near the end of his term in office, Richard D. Lamm of Colorado—who earned the sobriquet "Governor Gloom" for his unsentimental journeys into the future—began one of his speeches with the following parable: The U.S. fleet is on the high seas. Suddenly a blip appears on the radar screen. "Tell that ship to change its course 15 degrees," barks the admiral. The radio man complies, only to be signaled back, "You change *your* course 15 degrees." Incensed, the admiral gets on the radio himself. "I am an admiral in the U.S. Navy. Change your course 15 degrees at once." The word comes back: "You change *your* course 15 degrees. I am a lighthouse."

Summing up what he had learned during twelve years as governor, Lamm draws this moral: "Beware of solutions appropriate to the past but disastrous to the future." Or, as the old hymn reminds us: "New occasions teach new duties, time makes ancient good uncouth."

If the nuclear arms race offers the ultimate specter of competing virtues triggering potentially deadly consequences, there are many others. In an age of interdependence, the old virtues—in fact, any virtue possessed as an attainment rather than shared as a community good—directly threatens us all.

In an interdependent age, the question is not, "What can I do to be saved?" but, "What can we do to save one another?" Whenever our possession of something (even justice, faith, love, and truth) denies others access to it (selective justice, militant faith, exclusive love, dogmatic truth) we become traitors, subverting the commonwealth of God.

Not that individuals must refrain from competing. When great achievements in sport or science ennoble the entire human community, they possess a sacramental quality.

Contrast the downing of the Korean airliner and Plato's chariot of fire with the fiery explosion of the space shuttle *Challenger.*

By any rational measure, the death of seven people, even on a mission such as this one, should not have the power to displace all other world news from our minds, but for a time it did. This tragedy gathered us from our individual pursuits, uniting us as participants in a single, poignant moment in the drama of human history.

Such moments occur on but 'a handful of occasions in the lifetime of any generation. When they do, human events assume a mythic quality. In death, the seven astronauts became larger than life. This was not only because the news media exploited this story, overwhelming us with details, flooding us with heart-rending images, though surely they played their part. In an age of global communications, dramas such as this one, which before in our history would have only local or regional impact, touch lives all around the globe.

Myths project individual realities upon a cosmic screen. They are not fantasies, but larger-than-life visions by which our lives may be better understood. By such a measure, the story of the ill-fated *Challenger* mission is rich in mythic material. Three of the elements common to one well-known mythic pattern are present: the sacrifice of individuals on behalf of the many; the elevation of a common person, an everyman or everywoman, to heroic status; and a noble mission or adventure to expand our horizons and unite us, by the proxy of the hero or heroes, in a high and shared endeavor.

A handful of people, everyman and everywoman, ventured into space, and though, through no fault of their own, they failed in their mission they succeeded in uniting, if only for a moment, a divided people and divided world. Even the Soviets named two craters on Venus in honor of the two American women who died. Invested by their sacrifice with a new sense of human dignity, we were ennobled by the nobility of the victims, an ennobling made all the more powerful, in fact, only made possible, by their essential similarity to each of us. We were arrested from our pettiness to ponder the nature of heroism. These men and women inspired us to recommit ourselves in small but significant ways. They challenged us to serve and to care, especially to risk, fearing loss far less than the ultimate meaninglessness of a life lived without the risk of loss.

Here fortitude became a shared virtue. This was especially true of Christa McAuliffe, a public school teacher who captured the hearts of so many. But consider the entire crew: men and women; married and single; mothers and fathers; black, oriental and white; Christian, Jew, and Buddhist; professional and nonprofessional; Americans from Kansas, New Hampshire, North Carolina, Utah, New York, Maryland, and Hawaii; everyman and everywoman.

As religious creatures we were impelled, not to embrace some particular creed or body of religious dogma, but to contemplate the meaning of our lives and deaths in whatever ways we can. In such contemplation we enter into the mythic, or transrational realm, reaching for universals, seeking guides, and longing for heroes to chart a higher way.

Sadly, we live in an age almost bereft of heroes. But we do not, indeed cannot, live in a world bereft of myth, even though some myths are destructive. On the political stage, our skepticism and experience may lead us to resist the

allure of larger-than-life champions, but we compensate by
fearing larger than life enemies. This imbalance is dangerous precisely because it inspires us to act, not in obedience
to love, but in response to fear, which leads to hate.

Our desperate need for heroes clearly fed the national
paroxysm of grief in the wake of the shuttle tragedy. We
placed a greater burden on the shoulders of these seven
Americans than the reality of their lives could reasonably
bear. But myths—noble or ignoble, illuminating or de-
meaning—transcend the realm of fact. They deal with the
meanings behind individual words and deeds. If our hun-
ger for heroes in part explains the national mourning that
followed upon the death of these seven astronauts, this was
simply because we discovered in their deaths an emptiness
in our own lives. The fireball which riveted us time and
again to our television screens became a sacrament, a redemptive communion, a vicarious passion. Participating in
it, we too reached out to touch the stars.

The stars.

Here is the final piece of this myth: to touch the face of
God, moving beyond ourselves into a new realm of en-
counter and discovery. "Ah, but a man's reach should exceed his grasp, or what's a heaven for?" Robert Browning
asked. Or, as the President of the United States said in his
beautiful and inspiring message to the schoolchildren of
America, "Sometimes painful things like this happen. It's
all part of taking a chance and expanding man's horizons."

Ronald Reagan was not speaking here of American horizons, but human horizons. One undeniable gift of space
travel is that the farther we venture from the earth, the
clearer it becomes that ultimately all human horizons are
the same.

7. The Poetry of God

> Small as is our whole system compared with the infinitude of creation, brief as is our life compared with the cycles of time, we are so tethered to all by the beautiful dependencies of law, that not only the sparrow's fall is felt to the outermost bound, but the vibrations set in motion by the words that we utter reach through all space and the tremor is felt through all time.
>
> MARIA MITCHELL (NINETEENTH-CENTURY ASTRONOMER)

The day before the *Challenger* burst into flames, my wife Amy and I flew back from Lima, Peru, to the United States on the *Concord.* God had called me to spend my vacation lecturing about the devil on an ocean liner, and one of the two of them provided free passage home on this marvelous plane.

We flew at twice the speed of sound, sixteen hundred miles an hour, at sixty thousand feet. When we broke the sound barrier, I couldn't exactly feel it, but I sensed that something remarkable had happened. It may seem silly, but at the time I felt that I had entered another dimension, or—perhaps better—that the dimension of my being had been expanded. People tell me that if one travels regularly on the *Concord* this sensation becomes routine. Given how easily we become jaded, I fear they may be right.

One of the reasons that the *Challenger* disaster shocked us so was precisely because space travel *had* become routine, a commonplace of daily life. That this is true no longer represents the final gift bequeathed to us by the seven martyred astronauts.

To thrive, we must do everything in our power to ensure

that our lives not become routine, because far more awe-some than the entry into space is the exploration of life itself, of which space exploration is only a tiny part. Symbolically it is an important part. It expands our horizons by giving us a new perspective, a worldview in the literal sense upon the earth as a single organism, a home which we share as members of a single if divided family. But the real adventure lies not in space but on earth, where the mystery to be explored is our own world of invisible connections, matter and energy spun into life-sustaining patterns. Everything that exists is related, tracing its genesis to the instant of universal creation. We too are star-stuff, woven into an infinitely complex organism.

This insight has enormous and potentially redemptive consequence. "Spiritual men and women in the future will regard existence increasingly as an indivisible unity, wholly worldly and self-sufficient, yet at the same time of a depth that invites further exploration," writes Louis Dupré. Today the cutting edge of such exploration is carried on by scientists, not theologians. Religion's task is to turn knowledge into wisdom. Where the old models have failed us, the new offer hope. Here science is not theology's enemy, but its handmaiden.

Drawing from evidence garnered by science, Holmes Rolston III writes, "In our 150 pounds of protoplasm, in our three pounds of brain, there may be more operational organization than there is in the whole of the Andromeda Galaxy. The number of associations possible among our 10 billion neurons, and hence the number of thoughts humans can think, may exceed the number of atoms in the universe. Humans, too, are stars in the show." In and of itself, this should be enough to inspire awe, the primal religious emotion.

It also suggests, more persuasively than any human scripture, the work of a divine architect. "Like the man who survives execution by a 1,000-gun firing squad, we are entitled to suspect that there is some reason we are here, that perhaps there is a Friend behind the blast," Rolston concludes. He underestimates the odds. Modern cosmologists used to reckon the chances of human life as billions to one. Today, according to James Gleick, "They toss around numbers like 10^{40}, or 10^{301}, or 10 to the 10 to the 30th, a number that cannot even be typeset without either two levels of superscript or a universe full of zeroes."

Taken alone, this might not force us to reexamine our theologies, but the unfolding nature of the creation and our place in it inevitably must. Scientists can't do this for us. To cite Haldane's Law, "The universe is not only queerer than we imagine, it's queerer than we *can* imagine." But discoveries on the cutting edge of science can provide new metaphors to help us better understand our relationship to God and one another.

Truth in religion is like truth in poetry. Our common text is the creation. Though limited by the depth and field of our vision, we are driven to make sense of it as best we can. So we tell stories, formulate hypotheses, develop schools of thought and worship, pass our partial wisdom down from generation to generation. Not only every religion, but every philosophy, ideology, and scientific worldview is critical school with the creation of its text. We are all interpreters of the poetry of God.

Compare this with literary criticism. How various are the ways which we read a masterpiece. A great piece of literature admits to many levels of interpretation: literal, metaphorical, analogical, symbolic, political, structural, moral. Two critics may arrive at radically different interpretations of the same passage, both founding their views on carefully reasoned logic and demonstrating impressive erudition in the course of their proof. Within any given school of criticism a continuing discussion takes place, sharpening perspectives, issuing in new and relevant discoveries, all of which help to illuminate the nature of the masterpiece. And between schools as well there exists the possibility of dialogue occasionally promoting a new, more dynamic view from each of two distinctive perspectives.

The same thing holds for competing theologies. But compounding the level of difficulty, here the common text is the creation, the greatest masterpiece of them all. Interpreters with differing approaches, methodologies, and tools struggle to discover who we are, where we have come from, how we got here, where we are heading, and why and how. Each works from a set of basic presuppositions; each has its trusted tools, such as scientific method, dialectic, revelation. And, as among literary critics, there is an ongoing discussion within each school and occasional dialogue between schools. Religions adapt to new discoveries in science. Scientists sometimes reach the point of furthest penetration and adopt the mystical language of reverence and adoration.

The stakes are high. Of all intellectual contests, none is more charged, or dangerous. Each side reckons the score in a different fashion and there is no mutually accepted guideline for who is winning, or how to play. Viewed as competition, the only way to secure a final victory is to eliminate one's opponents, either by converting, ignoring, or destroying them.

Much of the time we remain spectators in these great contests, yet every once in a while even the most passive among us is cast into the interpretive task. A loved one dies. A marriage collapses. We are given three months to live. Something awakens us, knocking us off our pins, hurling us headlong into a confrontation with reality. Back and forth we go between our workaday lives and the abyss, drawing a little knowledge here, a little comfort there, trying to put it all together in a way that makes some sense. Then, to convince ourselves that we are right, we try to convince others that what makes sense to us ought to make sense to them.

The questions we ask of the creation are life-and-death questions. Accordingly, the answers are emotionally charged. It is hard to accept that if we are right, others who have differing views can be anything but wrong. This attitude leads to such things as Christian imperialism and Marxist manifest destiny, indeed to every imaginable form of intimidation, all carried out under the banner of truth.

But if there can be many arguable interpretations of a poem, what should this tell us about the cosmos itself? Nothing is more mysterious nor more veiled than the secret of creation. No single dogma can begin to comprehend it. Even as a scientific investigator cannot measure the velocity and mass of a particle at the same time, the moment we begin to parse the creation we change its nature. Gestalt psychology suggests a like point in object-and-field studies such as that well-known optical illusion of two faces in profile which also outline the shape of a vase. It is possible to go back and forth from one focus to another, but, though each is before our very eyes, we can't see both the faces and the vase at once. In each instance, the investigator becomes part of the experiment, affecting the very data he or she is attempting objectively to collect.

Not only are we the interpreters of God's poetry, we are the poem itself.

This doesn't mean that the search for truth or knowledge is vain. In fact, discoveries such as the Heisenburg Uncertainty Principle—pointing out that the experimenter affects the data—are breakthroughs in knowledge. And it doesn't mean that all truths are relative, and therefore functionally interchangeable, only that no truth is final.

There has never been a time when this wasn't so. We create our pictures of God by distilling our own understandings and experiences of power, whether physical, technological, societal, or spiritual, and then projecting these upon a cosmic screen.

When we were hunters and gatherers, living in caves and at the mercy of the elements, God was coterminous with nature, manifest in thunder and lightning, rising with the sun and moon, dancing in the wind, felt in the force of a volcano.

Later, when we turned to horticulture for our survival, this animistic faith evidenced itself in a new form, the procreative Goddess, mother of creation, who blessed the sowing and the reaping, signifying the life-sustaining, or withholding, power of the seasons, and vagaries of the weather.

As human society became yet more complicated, theology followed. The notion of God's transcendence began to supplant that of God's immanence. The gods became kings, each his people's guardian, emblematic of the new paternalistic structure of authority.

And then there was only one king, Lord of creation, all people children of one father, all creatures born of one creator. God the creator formed this earth, fixed the stars in the firmament, fashioned life, and ruled as almighty judge of his handiwork. In large measure, this is the Judeo-Christian God: transcendent, immaterial, immutable, condescending, just, demanding, and often even cruel. Under God's aegis, the world which once embodied God became the devil's playground, worldly things leaden and sinful, the earth itself an arena of temptation from which the motivated spirit strives to escape, returning intact to God.

This notion of an almighty, transcendent, distant, and judgmental deity is reflected in the traditional soul-body dualism which distinguishes so much Christian teaching. Our soul is said to be trapped in our body, struggling against the temptations of the flesh. Salvation, therefore, becomes an individual quest. If the soul can triumph over the flesh, the hope remains that upon our death, or with the end of the world when the devil's kingdom is overthrown, we shall be liberated from the tyranny of the crass, material realm and united with our maker on divine ground.

With the Copernican revolution, for many thoughtful people this cart was overturned. Displaced from the center of the universe, our image of God underwent another transformation, suggesting a metaphor that suited itself to this new worldview: God the watchmaker, who created the world, wound it up, set it ticking, and then withdrew to another corner of the universe. This is the god of the Deists—still transcendent but no longer personal—icy and remote.

Today, we are witness to yet another scientific revolution, one as profound as that initiated by Copernicus half a millennium ago. Put in terms of God's immanence or transcendence, we have moved from the immanent gods and goddesses of nature to a transcendent God, first Lord and judge, then absentee architect. Now, what emerges is a reflexive God, cocreator with us in unfolding, intricate drama of hitherto unimaginable complexity. This God is not immutable, not unchanging, but ever-changing, reaching, and growing, even as we change and reach and grow. No longer actors, we are participants in God's drama.

More sharply to distinguish the features of transcendent and reflexive divinity, reflect upon three contrasting images drawn from optical technology: the magnifying glass, the prism, and the holograph.

With a magnifying glass, on a sunny day you can go outdoors, focus the otherwise imperceptible rays of the sun on some dry leaves, and they will catch fire. The rays of the sun beat down everywhere, of course, but lacking the focus offered by the glass they are not transformed into a tangible power that can ignite tinder into burning ash.

According to this model, two things are required for God's power to evidence itself. First, the human soul must be prepared. Even as wet leaves would not ignite in response to the focusing of the sun's rays, an unreceptive soul would prove immune to the outpouring of God's grace. Second, God's presence must be focused. In traditional Christian parlance, the magnifying glass which focuses God's presence upon a receptive soul is the gospel.

This metaphor offers a "hot" model of the way God might become manifest to the human soul. It also explains why God's presence is not universally felt across all of human experience. God is with us always, but lacking focus and our own receptivity, we lack evidence. On the other hand, those who do experience God through the glass of the gospel are set afire by the holy spirit and transformed, even as the dry leaves are ignited and transformed by the focusing of the sun's rays through a magnifying glass.

The prism offers a different, cooler, model, by which God—still transcendent—might be experienced objectively and not subjectively. Here the light is caught by the prism and broken into its component parts. These too are not evident without the aid of an instrument, in this case not the gospel but the human mind, through which life's manifold appearances are filtered in search of some pattern to explain not only their complexity, but also their symmetry and orderliness.

The cool model has long been a favorite among rationalists. During the Enlightenment, it led to the argument from design. Focused through the prism of thought, the spectrum of reality was perceived as so intricate and orderly as to demand the original efforts of a creative mind.

Thomas Jefferson held this view. Upon the discovery of mammoth skeletons, he and his enlightened friends lavished a considerable amount of money and effort searching for mammoths in North America, basing their confidence on the conviction that mammoths could not be extinct or the perfect balance of God's dispensation—which demanded a living mammoth in the west for every elephant in the east—would be unimaginably disrupted.

If the hot view of God tends, in the West at least, toward a personal God who invokes a pietistic response in the hearts of his children, the cool view elicits a distant and respectful reverence for a much more impersonal divine master of ceremonies. By worshiping this God, many of my own Unitarian forbears earned the epithet (now shared with Episcopalians) of "God's frozen people."

The third image, that of the holograph, is both hot and cool; but it differs from these other models even as they resemble one another, offering a reflexive rather than transcendent image for God. The holograph works in conjunction with a laser, which records images on a photoplate made up of thousands of tiny lenses. The result is a three-dimensional hologram, like those you may have seen in the Haunted House at Disneyland, or on your charge card. Mysteriously, if the photo-plate is broken to bits and only a single shard of the original is employed for projection, though faint the entire image will be replicated.

Our bodies too are holographic: each of our cells contains the full genetic coding for our whole being, itself an even more telling metaphor for the reflexive nature of God: *The Realm of God is in a mustard seed; the Father and I are one; Atman (individual consciousness) and Brahman (universal consciousness) are one; the realm of God is within you.*

As with Paul's image of the cosmic Christ (one body, many members, each with the same signature of divinity), the holograph suggests God's reflexive nature in a way that transforms our relationship not only with God, but with one another as well. "The religion of the future will be a cosmic religion," Albert Einstein writes. "Covering both the natural and the spiritual, it should be based on a religious sense arising from the experience of all things, as a meaningful unity."

For this vision, epiphanies abound. They always have.

In 1899, Vincent van Gogh opened the door of the asylum at St. Rémy, beheld the firmament—"The Starry Night"—and saw a masterpiece: nature trembling, dancing with energy; matter swirling, pulsating; star-stuff; an orange crescent moon; the sensuous purple hills; and a simple village church, its steeple reaching tentatively into the vivid sky.

In 1926, Admiral Richard Byrd gazed out upon an Antarctic sunset near the Bay of Whales, the day dying, the night being born, and heard the music of the spheres: "It was enough to catch that rhythm, momentarily, to be myself a part of it. In that instant I could feel no doubt of man's oneness with the universe. . . . It was a feeling that transcended reason; that went to the heart of man's despair and found it groundless. The universe was a cosmos, not a chaos."

And in 1946, Austrian author Hans Habe, interned by the Nazis during the war, having arrived in America, ventured out one silvery evening, the sky gleaming like a frozen lake, to greet "the passers-by . . . the houses on the road, the cows in the pastures, the butterflies in the air; the earth that was fragrant and the heavens that were so close to me. I tried to find someone whom I could help. Never was anyone in rags so rich."

Three nights, not unlike every night.

Three epiphanies.

8. Pentecost in Purgatory

Someday after mastering the winds, the waves, the tides and gravity, we shall harvest for God the energies of love, and then for the second time in the history of the world we shall have discovered fire.

PIERRE TEILHARD DE CHARDIN

Jonah didn't want to be a prophet. As is so often the case, where there are many openings few apply. It's hard to blame him. A true prophet must suffer. So when God called Jonah, and said to him, "Arise and go to the great city of Nineveh, go now and denounce it, for its wickedness stares me in the face," Jonah booked passage on the next ship out, not to Nineveh but in precisely the opposite direction.

Ironically, it is during his flight from God, not his later service, that Jonah displays his regard for humanity. His ship runs into high seas and then a mighty storm. White-capped waves crash over the bow. Should the storm continue, the ship will surely go down. Clearly the gods are angry, and soon all eyes turn to Jonah. "Who are you?" the Phonecian sailors cry. "Where do you come from? What have you done wrong?"

"I am a Hebrew," Jonah replies. "And I worship the God of heaven, who made both sea and land. It is my fault that the sea has risen against you. God called upon me and I tried to flee from God." Here Jonah demonstrates true virtue. "You must throw me overboard," he tells them, "and the sea will go down." Over Jonah goes, and at once the sea grows calm. The ship is saved, and Jonah is swallowed by a great fish.

For three days, deep within the belly of the fish, Jonah prays to God, offering up his thanks and promising to pay his vows should God give him a second chance. His prayers are answered. The fish vomits Jonah up on the beach. Having thought he learned his lesson, Jonah travels straight to Nineveh and denounces its crimes, proclaiming that in forty days Nineveh will be destroyed.

But then something wonderful happens. The people listen; their king decrees a period of penitence; and God spares Nineveh.

Jonah, of course, is furious. He had done his duty, proclaiming the righteous word of God's vengeful justice, and nothing happened. He felt a fool, his honor tarnished. Jonah placed his reputation on the line, but God didn't deliver. Not to mention the fact that justice was not done. So what does Jonah do? He goes out and sits down on the east of the city and sulks.

Displaying a divine sense of humor, God ordains that a climbing gourd should grow up over Jonah's head to shade him from the sun. Jonah is grateful for the gourd, but at dawn the next day a worm attacks the gourd and it withers. Like the fires of purgatory, designed to burn away our self-deceit, the sun beats down on Jonah's head. But Jonah will not abandon his newfound virtue. Growing faint, he offers up a final desperate prayer to God, this time for death.

They say that virtue has few martyrs, but Jonah almost makes it. He is prepared to die for justice, not the justice God dispenses, but the tooth-for-a-tooth variety that he, a prophet, so passionately proclaimed in Nineveh.

In the course of this brief story, Jonah falls twice—first on account of selfishness, and then self-righteousness. The first time, a sinner, Jonah acts valiantly, offering his life to save others; later, a messenger of God, he plays the cad, whining that he wants to die because others had been spared. "The wise turns vices into virtues; the fool, virtues into vices," as the old adage goes. Thinking little of himself, Jonah proves his wisdom; when puffed up with virtue, he demonstrates his folly.

But having saved the people of Nineveh despite their sins, God will not permit Jonah to destroy himself for virtue. Instead God asks this leading question: "Are you so angry over the gourd?"

"Yes," Jonah answers, "mortally angry."

"Think about it, Jonah. You are sorry to lose the gourd, though you did not have the trouble of growing it, a plant which came up in a night and withered in a night. How is it then that I should not be sorry for the great city of Nineveh, with its hundred and twenty thousand who cannot tell their right hand from their left, and cattle without number?" (Jonah 1–4).

So ends the Book of Jonah. You will notice that everyone is saved: The sailors from Jonah; Jonah from the sea; and the people of Nineveh, themselves not Jews, by the God of the Jews.

No wonder Jonah is so perplexed, for this marks a profound change in the nature of the divine dispensation. God's mercy extends not only to a chosen righteous few, but to all the earth's creatures, Gentile and Jew alike and cattle without number.

If the fall was an individual act, redemption turns out to be a corporate enterprise.

In Greek, the word for faith is related to a verb meaning to trust, or yield to; in Latin, the word for religion means to bind up, or tie together. Paradoxically, to strike a balance between the two we must remain off balance, never fixing in one spot but constantly shifting perspectives in order to gain a wider vision, a parallax view. This is why I address each of the three books that comprise this trilogy to both atheists and true believers, inviting the true believer to believe beyond God; and the doubter to doubt his or her disbelief.

The key is paradox, a word stemming from the Greek root *doxis,* meaning "right opinion." Dogma has the same etymology. But yesterday's right opinions are not necessarily tomorrow's. The world changes and we change with it. Literally, paradox means "contrary to right opinion." Its strange logic challenges us to turn things upside down, in order that we may view reality in more inclusive, less guarded ways.

As William of Baskerville concludes in *The Name of the Rose,* "Perhaps the mission of those who love mankind is to make people laugh at the truth, *to make truth laugh,* because the only truth lies in learning to free ourselves from our insane passion for the truth."

To adapt an old metaphor, each of us has two eyes (or I's): one divine, enabling us to see through the eyes of others; the other blind, through which we see others only as means to our own ends. Virtues we possess and claim as our own are blind virtues, deadly especially in an age of interdependence when survival hinges upon an expanded worldview, with others perceived not as means to our ends, but as ends in themselves. In contrast, our divine eye offers a parallax vision, permitting us to view the same object from different angles. This places virtue in a new light as something we share, not something we possess.

Since all virtues are community property, the community

in which the good is achieved has to be one of reconciliation. The theological counterpart to the adage, "Choose your enemies carefully because you will become like them," is "Love your enemies."

We spend a goodly amount of time squinting at the world through our blind eye. Our hope—not blind hope, but a hope that may be shared—is to discover this before it is too late, both for our neighbors and ourselves.

This may require a leap of faith in our religious communities, where one truth so often is set up in opposition to another. It also calls for a major shift in emphasis among our secular shamans, therapists who prescribe competitive virtues as a tonic to enhance individual self-esteem, and reformers who preach that to dismantle the master's house, we must use the master's tools. As Ruth Tiffany Barnhouse writes,

From the religious point of view, we have not understood that every member of the entire human family is our neighbor; much less have we approached them primarily on the basis of real care for their welfare, and respect for their chosen ways.

From the psychiatric point of view, it is not possible to unleash *selectively* the primitive aggression necessary to acquire and maintain power over others, even in a "good cause." The ends not only do not justify the means, but aggressive means can subvert even the best of ends.

If the only pain in life that has meaning is shared pain, the one true joy is shared joy. Whether material or spiritual, exclusively held properties possess only illusionary value, whereas mutual goods credit everyone by enhancing the commonweal. The former are illusionary, for we are inextricably linked to one another in an interdependent web of being. In the commonwealth of God, goods are held in common, because there is no other way in which goods can be held.

This is the new truth, though many old prophets have spoken it. All of us are part of one body, even those who never awaken to the nature of our interdependencies. We may spend our lives as antibodies within the body of Christ— or Atman or God or the universe—but still, whatever sustenance we may garner springs from this common source. When we squander our lives we squander life itself; when we give our lives away to others we enhance all life, including our own.

Samuel Beckett wrote a play called *Trapp's Last Tape,* about a man who celebrated the end of every year by dictating his successes and accomplishments on tape while they were fresh in mind. At the end of his sixty-ninth year, Trapp decides to try something different. He plays all the old tapes over again.

As he listens, he discovers something about his life he had never noticed before. The memories that stand out, that give him greatest pleasure and in retrospect appear most meaningful, are not his victories, promotions, or private coups against some long-forgotten adversary. Instead they are moments of profound, almost mystical, connectedness when momentarily he became part of all he loved.

Jesus said that the realm of God is within us. But the Greek preposition *entos,* which is translated here as "within," also means two other things: "between" and "among." When we open our divine eye—perceiving the myriad connections within us, between us, and among us, and becoming a part of all we see—we enter the commonwealth of God.

No longer deadly and blind, here the virtues of love and

justice are saving virtues. The Latin root from which our word "salvation" stems means "good health." Our Tuetonic words "whole," "holy," "hale," and "health" are intimately related as well. And "Salam/shalom," meaning "peace," stems from the Semitic root meaning "whole." Wholeness is peace, and salvation is health. Sin, on the other hand, is the condition of fragmentation, alienation, estrangement, and brokenness.

This is the human condition. In purgatory, we submit to the pain that comes with self-recognition. Here—at once broken yet sustained by the promise of wholeness, estranged yet powered by the hope of reconciliation, alienated yet drawn to the embrace of God's love—we are schooled in self-acceptance and forgiveness, which liberates us to perform the work of God on earth. In the commonwealth of God, each act of reconciliation is a token of salvation.

At times this seems impossible. Esteemed virtues, secular totems, and brazen idols compete daily for our allegiance. All of us cloak ourselves in virtues that set us apart from others, even as we succumb to the principalities and powers that tyrannize our world and threaten its destruction. But when the fires of heaven illumine the landscape of our souls, paradoxically, through God's grace, it is because of, not despite our own sinfulness that we become aware of the nature of our relationship with others. By accepting self-acceptance, to use Paul Tillich's phrase, we participate in wholeness. Our lives become sacraments of praise.

Yet our confidence in the old values, based upon virtues promoting self-enhancement and tribal security, subverts recognition of our interdependencies. A larger faith, multiform yet multilateral, based upon yet transcending a host of particular expressions, is undercut daily by a powerful cadre of competitive faiths, each in its own way deadly. Entering their champions into the lists (zealots inspired by scripture and prepared to kill and die for truth), competing faiths crucify God—greater than all and yet present in each—in God's name.

Religious or otherwise, every war between peoples, parties, or faiths is a civil war, brothers and sisters killing one another with words or weapons, renting the one fabric, riving the body of God. This is why we so desperately need new metaphors to illustrate the interdependent nature of all life, images that will awaken us to our kinship with one another, allowing for distinctive beliefs, while offering a canopy underneath which all belief, howsoever disparate, may reside.

Reducing all beliefs to a lowest common denominator will not work, nor would it be worthy if it did. Bleeding religions of their particularity would only drain them of their nutrients. Each faith has its particular strength, drawn from history and prophecy, from shared reflection upon life's meaning and common patterns of worship that together invest its symbols and message with saving power. Because of this, every religion sponsors values different from every other, in some cases strikingly so. Anyone who talks glibly of one religion for all people has little religion to begin with.

The commonwealth of God is grounded not in uniformity but mutuality. We are not replicates of one another, distinctive only to the extent that we have or have not received Jesus as our Lord and Savior, but related to one another in a single body with many different members, each with a unique gift. Which means, among other things, that converting a Jew to Christianity is like trying to turn a hand into a foot.

Members in the commonwealth of God are not bound together by the specifics of their religion, for the nature of our interdependency does not require this. Rather we are bound by the shared recognition that when one person suffers, all suffer; when we violate one life, all lives are violated; when we pollute the earth, all living things are stained; when one nation threatens the security of another, it too becomes less secure; when we place the planet in mortal danger, we hazard the future of our own children as well as the children of our enemies.

"Coin tossing becomes our primary metaphor for resolution," as Stephen Jay Gould writes. We are left with a win/lose rather than a win/win approach to conflict resolution. "The truly great intellectual dichotomies are not battles to the death, but struggles to find the partial truths of each vision," he concludes. "If we tried a large set of twofold divisions, placing the wall of separation at different angles and in different places each time, we might finally occupy enough perspectives to appreciate the true complexity of most issues."

Defining virtue in a cooperative rather than competitive fashion, the good we seek is the common good, moving wherever possible from "either/or" confrontation to "both/and" reconciliation. This is Paul's model in Romans. It is the goal of arms negotiation. It can be practiced within our homes and our churches, between nations, and among the world's religions.

It is pentecost in purgatory.

In the Book of Acts the Holy Spirit descends upon the

disciples' heads as tongues of fire—the agent of illumination and purification, that burns away impediments to mutual understanding—translating their good news into language that all people, regardless of tongue or dialect, can understand.

Pentecost is the feast day of the Holy Spirit. If God the Father is the ancient image for God's transcendence, and God the Son, of God's immanence, the Holy Spirit, moving among and between us, is emblematic of the reflexive nature of God. Expressed in tongues of fire, the holy spirit doesn't quell distinctiveness, but facilitates understanding among peoples.

Pentecost in purgatory offers a like promise: fire dancing upon every head, enabling us to understand, despite our differing languages and even differing beliefs, that all of us are part of the body of God, interdependent upon, with, and for one another, and responsible for one another's well-being as if it were our own.

Remember, according to the Bible all sins may be forgiven, with this one exception: sins "against the Holy Spirit." Such sins are not only committed against God, but also against our neighbor and ourself. Pentecost in purgatory awakens us to love God and our neighbor as ourselves, because in essence, we, God, and our neighbor are one.

This doesn't mean we should let our neighbor run all over us. Taking the body metaphor seriously, such would be suicide. In extreme instances, we may even be driven to follow the hard injunction of Jesus, and when our right eye offends us, pluck it out. We do as much with our own bodies when cancer strikes. We don't honor the cancer simply because it is part of us, for it preys within, imperiling the whole.

The weakness of liberal theology, reflected in modern society at large, is that in recognizing the plurality of distinctive approaches and the diversity of independent value systems, we abandon all faith in norms for behavior. This fragments virtue into a multiplicity of independent and self-affirming value systems. Such value systems exist and always will. But far more is required than mere tolerance.

Those who are addicted to alcohol or drugs are able to tolerate the poison that is destroying them in greater and greater quantities. The same thing holds for an uncritical or nonjudgmental tolerance for other peoples' values. Today our very survival depends upon the establishment of a new norm by which to judge all such values, or virtues.

That norm is the commonweal.

Most fundamentalists would define this norm according to their own narrow strictures and, imposing it, inflict their own values on everyone. In an age of interdependence this is heresy. But to avoid this heresy, we mustn't abandon the quest for communitarian values and cooperative virtue, even if it leads to a vigorous intolerance of groups or individuals who, in the name of freedom, truth, or God, place the common good in jeopardy.

Though the foundations for cooperative virtue, and a relational approach to conflict resolution are established in scripture, and demonstrated by science, as of today little building has taken place upon them. As Gould writes, "I despair of persuading people to stop playing dichotomy; the need seems to lie too deep in the human soul."

Yet we seem to have an instinct for survival. For centuries this instinct has been tutored by the imperatives of ethnocentrism. Defending such imperatives, Allan Bloom writes in *The Closing of the American Mind,* "Men must love and be loyal to their families and their peoples in order to preserve them. Only if they think their own things are good can they rest content with them."

His brilliant defense of the competitive virtues has only one flaw. In a nuclear age, to preserve our families and our peoples, we must struggle somehow to preserve our enemies' families and their peoples. "The problem of getting along with outsiders is secondary to, and sometimes in conflict with, having an inside, a people, a culture, a way of life," he writes. But today, in an age of interdependence, there are no outsiders, not really.

Since there is no meaning apart from particularity, we must continue to preserve our existential distinctiveness, while finding ways to reorient our instinct for survival that we may recognize and act upon our essential kinship and common peril.

This is the promise of purgatory. Here we—who otherwise are alienated from life itself, torn from the fabric of being, alone in the cosmos—are invited to oneness with God. Seeing through our divine eye, we find paths toward reconciliation with those from whom we are estranged, loved ones whom we so often are tempted to hate, neighbors whose plight we are inured to and ignore, coworkers grating on our nerves or competing for our turf, people not of our faith or color or sex or sexual orientation or political creed. Yes, even our enemies, whom Jesus teaches us to love.

Pilgrims in purgatory, we discover our true mission: to make peace in a war-torn world, to affirm the kinship of all people, and serve as stewards of the earth, this hospitable planet that is our home.

From personal experience, I know how difficult the transition from our own willful domination to the commonwealth of God can be. In fact, when reading Carol Gilligan's book and others like it, I recognize myself far more often in depictions of the old, dysfunctional, hierarchical value system, than I do in illustrations of a new relational and therefore potentially redemptive model for human interaction.

Compounding this, we converts to models based upon relationship are tempted to enjoin them in the old-fashioned way, and that won't work. This is why the purgatorial fires, whatever name we give to them, are so important. Most of us have a load of extra baggage to be burned. Having carried that baggage for years, this process is a painful one, but that's the way it is in purgatory. To become who we might be, we must sacrifice a part of who we are.

The word sacrifice means "to render sacred."

Epilogue

In the Greek Orthodox Church in the cool darkness of an early spring night, the celebration of Easter begins with the blessing of new fire. Struck from flint, this new fire passes from one candle to another until the church is filled with light.

I first learned of this ceremony when reading Thomas Merton. He describes how, long ago on Easter night, Russian peasants would carry the new fire home to their cottages from church. "The light would scatter and travel in all directions through the darkness," Merton writes, "and the desolation of the night would be pierced and dispelled as lamps came on in the windows of the farmhouses one by one."

Here, emerging from the darkness, out of deathly shadows, new fire, kindled from candle to candle, lights home after home.

Even darkness, even evil, even death, seen by the light of the sacramental fire . . . can contribute accidentally, but existentially, to the life, growth and liberty of our souls . . . And the night, then: the night of inertia, anguish and ignorance, . . . it is the passage through non-being into being, the recovery of existence from non-existence, the resurrection of life out of death.

That's the way it is with purgatory: the fires of heaven illumining the darkness of hell, the knowledge of salvation kindled by the sharing of both suffering and light. Citizens of the commonwealth of God, awakened to our promise after a long night of estrangement, we are woven into one another's mortal fabric and our lives and deaths have meaning once again. "Not till we are lost," writes Henry David Thoreau, "not till we have lost the world, do we begin to find ourselves, and realize where we are and the infinite extent of our relations."

The blessing of new fire in the Easter vigil has less to do with life after death than it does with the kindling of new life on earth. By entering the darkness, acknowledging and claiming it as our own, when the new fire is lit and blessed and passed, its blessing, uniting us with others, becomes our blessing. Our lives are purified in the fire of Christ's passion and triumph, not an individual victory, but a victory for us all.

Here on earth, this is perhaps the most we can hope for: Heaven and hell at once, stark in juxtaposition, perplexing yet inviting us to enter into the flames to undergo the pains of suffering with those who suffer, and to kindle our neighbors' candles throughout the earthly village; ours not the bright lights of virtue, but flickering tapers, each illumining the darkness first like a firefly and then the wick of a hearth lamp; light from darkness, good from evil, each a reminder that we must be in purgatory, for surely we are saved.

Benediction

First for you, my wife and children,
to me most close and dear,
for your joy and your anger,
your laughter and your tears,
your patience and your impatience,
for all the delight and all the bother
of being with you day and night
throughout the years we have to share,
for the ways you bless me
and the ways you torment me,
for loving me and hating me,
building me up and tearing me down,
purifying my life and incinerating my life
in the fires of your passion,
I thank God for you.

And for you, my friends and neighbors,
each and every one,
for your strengths and weaknesses,
generosity and pettiness,
courage in bearing pain and self-pity,
for your compliments and criticism,
just and unjust,
for your self-forgetting love
and unlovely self-absorption,
for all your healing and your hurting ways,
for all you do and fail to do,
I thank God for you.

And for this planet and its people I thank God,
for all the sweet and sordid dreams,
the pitched drama of birth and death,
hope and fear, awakening me
to life's strength and life's fragility.

And I thank God for shoot and bud
flower and leaf,
for nature's cycle of growth and decay,
seed to husk,
in all its gentle and terrible beauty.

I thank God for friend and stranger,
sun and rain,
peace and danger,
balm and pain,
for moon and stars and light and mind,
wind and darkness,
cloud and rock,
for the breath of life given and taken away,
and for the mystery that marks
our living and our dying days,
I offer up my thanks to God.

Sources

PREFACE

1   **"Evil disguised as"** F. Forrester Church, *The Devil &
Dr. Church: a Guide to Hell for Atheists and True-
Believers* (San Francisco: Harper & Row, 1986), x.

1   **"goodness disguised"** F. Forrester Church, *Entertaining Angels: a Guide to Heaven for Atheists and
True-Believers* (San Francisco: Harper & Row, 1987),
11.

2   **"If purgatory is"** Jean Pierre Camus, *The Spirit of St.
Francis de Sales,* VI. 6., cited in *The Book of Catho-
lic Quotations,* John Chapin, ed. (New York: Farrar,
Straus, and Cudahy, 1956), 743.

2   **"The pains of"** Dorothy Sayers, Introduction to
Dante's *The Divine Comedy—2: Purgatory* (Balti-
more: Penguin, 1955), 15.

3   **"we are just"** (image adapted from) Wallace Rob-
bins, *Meditations* (Boston: Unitarian Universalist
Christian Fellowship, 1978), 41.

3   **"Our crimes would"** William Shakespeare, *All's Well
That Ends Well,* IV, iii, 83.

4   **"*Evil* was literally"** Robert Hughes, *The Fatal Shore*
(New York: Alfred A. Knopf, 1987), 483.

4   **"the projection beyond . . . of divine love"** Catherine
of Genova, *Treatise on Purgatory,* cited in The New
Catholic Encyclopedia, Vol. II (New York: McGraw-
Hill, 1967), 256.

5   **"Of all people"** Alan Lightman, quoted by James

Gleick, "Science on the Track of God," *New York Times Magazine* (January 4, 1987), 22.

1. THE PROMISE OF PURGATORY

9 **"Of that second"** Dante, *Purgatorio* I, 4–5, tr. Lawrence Binyon, *The Portable Dante* (New York: Viking, 1947), 188.

9 **"And so, Mr."** Sydney Owenson Morgan, *O'Donnell: A National Tale,* vol. III, (New York: AMS Press, 1813), 47.

9–11 *"Go there . . . an infinite happiness"* Shane Leslie, *The Story of St. Patrick's Purgatory* (London: B. Herder, 1917), iv., 12, 62–63.

11 **"This fire consumes"** Origen, cited in *The Book of Catholic Quotations,* John Chapin, ed. (New York: Farrar, Straus, and Cudahy, 1956), 741.

12 **"There is no"** Beaumont and Fletcher, *Scornful Lady,* III, i (Norwood, NJ: Walter J. Johnson, Inc., 1972; reprint of 1616 ed.).

13 **"When in the"** Johan Tetzel, cited in *Dictionary of Quotations,* Berger Evans, ed. (New York: Delacourt, 1968), 460.

14 **"the new life"** Evelyn Underhill, *Mysticism* (London: Methuen, 1949), 217.

14 **"I have no doubt"** Geoffrey Chaucer, "The Knight's Tale," *The Canterbury Tales,* tr. Coghill (New York: Penguin, 1951), 54–55.

15 **"I'll purge, and"** William Shakespeare, *King Henry IV, Part I,* V, iv, 168–70.

20 **"in the different"** Carol Gilligan, *In a Different Voice* (Cambridge: Harvard University Press, 1982), 173.

21   **"In Hell, community"** Dorothy Sayers, Introduction
to Dante's *The Divine Comedy—2: Purgatory* (Balti-
more: Penguin, 1955), p. 20.

21   **"The concept of"** Carol Gilligan, *In a Different
Voice* (Cambridge: Harvard University Press, 1982),
173.

2.   SNARES OF VIRTUE

23   **"The man of superior"** *Tao Te Ching* 38, translated
by Wing-Tsit Chan, *A Source Book in Chinese Philosophy* (Princeton, N.J.: Princeton Unitversity, 1963),
158.

23   **"Be happy. Stay"** Vanna White, from an interview in
Newsday

24   **"Top quality, plush"** from a Wee Win Toys newspa-
per advertisement entitled "Christians! Now You Can
Have Your Own Business," Wee Win Toys, 15340 Van-
tage Pkwy, E., #250, Houston, Texas 77032.

27   **"Where virtue is"** John Chrysostom, *Homilies,* cited
in *The Book of Catholic Quotations,* John Chapin,
ed. (New York: Farrar, Straus, and Cudahy, 1956),
899.

27   **"Respectability, Childishness, Mental"** Dorothy L.
Sayers, *Creed or Chaos?* (London: Methuenx Co.
1947), 23.

27   **"Virtue itself turns"** William Shakespeare, *Romeo
and Juliet,* II, iii.

3.   TWO TYPES OF VIRTUE

29   **"The good of"** Thomas Aquinas, *Summa Contra
Gentiles,* chapter 71.

29 "[She] looked towards" Jan Struther, *Mrs. Miniver* (New York: Harcourt Brace, 1940), 48.

31 "**The difference is**" Alexander Pope, *Essay on Man,* 2.

33 "**Just when we**" Robert Browning, "The Grand Perhaps."

34–35 "**We'll begin at . . . a million years**" Thornton Wilder, *Our Town,* Act III (New York: Harper & Row/ Perennial, 1985), 93–101.

36 "**A society is**" Alasdair MacIntyre, *After Virtue* (Notre Dame, IN: Notre Dame, 1981), 232–33.

37 "**cooperative virtue,**" A. W. H. Adkins, *Merit and Responsibility* (London: Oxford University, 1960), 6.

38 "**What is alien . . . particularity and circumstance**" Alasdair MacIntyre, *After Virtue* (Notre Dame, IN: Notre Dame, 1981), 115, 157.

40 "**The nature of**" Thomas Aquinas, *Summa Theologica,* 1–2, 64, I.

41 "**The Antichrist can . . . of hell prevail**" Umberto Ecco, *The Name of the Rose* (San Diego: Harcourt Brace Jovanovich, 1983), 584, 598.

4. VIRTUE *ÜBER ALLES*

43 "**Every institution finally**" John Lord Acton, *The History of Freedom,* I. 3.

43 "**Fogarty, the only**" Mark Joseph, *To Kill the Potemkin* (New York: Onyx/New American Library, 1986), 182.

43–45 The idea for this adaptation of the Little Red Riding Hood story came to me courtesy of the Rev. Richard L. Allen, Unitarian Universalist minister in Oklahoma City.

46   **"This was very"** Kurt Vonnegut, Jr., "Address at Re-
      dedication of Wheaton College Library, 1973," *Wam-
      peters, Foma, & Granfalloons* (New York: Delacorte,
      1975), 213.

47–49 **"that spirit of . . . side of justice,"** for references
      see F. Forrester Church, "The First American Am-
      nesty Debate: Religion and Politics in Massachusetts,
      1783–1784," *Journal of Church and State,* volume
      21, number 1 (Winter 1979), 40, 46–50, 52.

50   **"George Williams, one"** Frank Church, *Parade Mag-
      azine,* cited by F. Forrester Church, *Father & Son: A
      Personal Biography of Senator Frank Church of
      Idaho by His Son* (New York: Harper & Row, 1985),
      99–100.

50–51 **"the love of . . . that we fought"** from the testi-
      mony of Lieutenant Colonel Oliver North before the
      Select Committee on Secret Military Assistance to
      Iran and to the Nicaraguan Opposition, as reprinted
      in *Taking the Stand* (New York: Pocket Books, 1987),
      256, 266, 267, 514.

51   **"Providence told Ollie"** Michael Novak, *Los Angeles
      Times* (July 14, 1987), II, 5.

51   **"a dedicated, patriotic"** Rep. Bill McCollum, *Taking
      the Stand,* 715.

51–52 **"the head of"** Robert Coles, "Middle America
      Knows the Score: Critics Smirk, but Millions See
      Their Own Values in the Norths," *Los Angeles Times*
      (July 26, 1987), V, 5.

52   **"the greatest dangers"** Justice William Brandeis,
      quoted by Senator Paul Sarbanes, *Taking the Stand,*
      580.

52   **"should we in"** Senator Daniel Inouye, *Taking the
      Stand,* 751.

5. PLAYING WITH FIRE

53 **"As far as"** Russell Hoban, *Pilgermann* (London: Jonathan Cape, 1983), 182.

58 **"always someone who . . . not private property"** Alasdair MacIntyre, *After Virtue* (Notre Dame, IN: Notre Dame, 1981), 213.

59 **"We need a"** Christopher Lasch, "Fraternalist Manifesto," *Harpers* (April 1987), 20.

62 **"Everything was seen"** Joseph Campbell, "Earthrise," *New York Times Magazine* (April 1979), 51.

6. CHARIOTS OF FIRE

65 **"Those times—those"** E. B. White, *The Second Tree from the Corner* (New York: Harper & Brothers, 1954), 69–70.

67 **"You know, I"** President Ronald Reagan, quoted by Anthony Lukas, in his review of A. G. Mojtabai, *Blessed Assurance* (Boston: Houghton Mifflin, 1986) in *The New York Times Book Review* June 8, 1986, 7.

69 **"Our virtues are"** La Rochefoucauld, *Maxims,* cited in *Familiar Quotations,* John Bartlett, ed., 14th Edition (Boston: Little, Brown: 1968), 354.

70 **"Tell that ship . . . to the future"** Richard D. Lamm, in an address presented to the Dallas Chamber of Commerce, December 2, 1986 (typescript), 1.

73 **"Ah, but a"** Robert Browning, "Andrea del Sarto," *Men and Women* (1855).

73 **"Sometimes painful things,"** President Ronald Reagan, White House Statement, Jan. 23, 1986.

7. THE POETRY OF GOD

75 **"Small as is,"** Maria Mitchell, quoted by Helen
Wright, *Sweeper in the Sky: The Life of Maria Mitch-
ell, First Woman Astronomer in America* (New York:
Macmillan, 1949), 227.

76 **"Spiritual men and"** Louis Dupré, "Spiritual Life in
a Secular Age," in *Religion and America: Spirituality
in a Secular Age,* ed. Mary Douglas and Steven Tip-
ton (Boston: Beacon Press, 1983), 13.

76 **"In our 150"** Holmes Rolston III, "Shaken Atheism:
A Look at the Fine-Tuned Universe," *The Christian
Century* (December 3, 1986), 1094.

77 **"They toss around"** James Gleick, "Science on the
Track of God," *New York Times Magazine* (April 1,
1987), 22.

77 **"The universe is"** Haldane's Law, in *The Official
Book of Rules,* ed. Paul Dickson (New York: Dela-
corte Press, 1978), 79.

84 **"The religion of"** Albert Einstein, *Cosmic Religion*
(New York: Covici-Friede, 1931), 1.

85 **"It was enough"** Admiral Richard E. Byrd, "A Cosmos, not a Chaos," *Alone* (New York: G. F. Putnam,
1938), 85.

85 **"the passers-by . . . the"** Hans Habe, in F. Forrester
Church, *Born Again Unitarian Universalism* (Tulsa:
Cone-Lewis, 1982), 93–94.

8.   PENTECOST IN PURGATORY

87   **"Someday after mastering"** Pierre Teilhard de Chardin, *The Divine Milieu,* (New York: Harper/Colophan, 1960), 144.

90   **"Perhaps the mission"** Umberto Ecco, *The Name of the Rose,* 598.

91   **"From the religious"** Ruth Tiffany Barnhouse, "The Vicissitudes of Reform," *Union Seminary Quarterly Review,* vol. 36 (Winter/Spring 1981), 138.

95   **"Coin tossing becomes . . . of most issues"** Stephen Jay Gould, "Archetype and Adaption," *Natural History* (October 1986), 16.

97   **"I despair of"** Stephen Jay Gould, "Archetype and Adaption," 16.

97–98   **"Men must love . . . way of life"** Allan Bloom, *The Closing of the American Mind* (New York: Simon and Schuster, 1987), 37.

EPILOGUE

101   **"The light would . . . out of death"** Thomas Merton, *The New Man* (New York: Farrer, Strauss (Udahy, 1961), 242.

102   **"Not till we"** Henry David Thoreau, *On Man and Nature* (Mt. Vernon, N.Y.: Peter Pauper Press, 1960), 15.